INVENTORS WHO CHANGED THE WORLD

LOUIS PASTEUR

THE FATHER OF MICROBIOLOGY

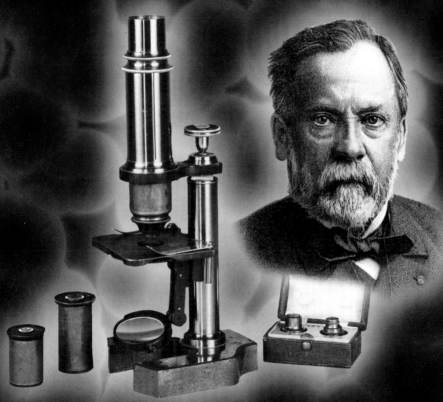

STEPHEN FEINSTEIN

MyReportLinks.com Books
an imprint of

 Enslow Publishers, Inc.
Box 398, 40 Industrial Road
Berkeley Heights, NJ 07922
USA

MyReportLinks.com Books, an imprint of Enslow Publishers, Inc. MyReportLinks®
is a registered trademark of Enslow Publishers, Inc.

Library of Congress Cataloging-in-Publication Data

Feinstein, Stephen.
  Louis Pasteur : the father of microbiology / Stephen Feinstein.
      p. cm. — (Inventors who changed the world)
  Includes bibliographical references and index.
  ISBN-13: 978-1-59845-078-1 (hardcover)
  ISBN-10: 1-59845-078-6 (hardcover)
  1. Pasteur, Louis, 1822–1895—Juvenile literature. 2. Scientists—France—Biography—
Juvenile literature. 3. Microbiologists—France—Biography—Juvenile literature. I. Title.
Q143.P2F45 2008
579.092—dc22
[B]
                                               2007006400

Printed in the United States of America

10 9 8 7 6 5 4 3 2 1

To Our Readers:
Through the purchase of this book, you and your library gain access to the Report Links that specifically back up this book.
The Publisher will provide access to the Report Links that back up this book and will keep these Report Links up to date on **www.myreportlinks.com** for five years from the book's first publication date.
We have done our best to make sure all Internet addresses in this book were active and appropriate when we went to press. However, the author and the Publisher have no control over, and assume no liability for, the material available on those Internet sites or on other Web sites they may link to.
The usage of the MyReportLinks.com Books Web site is subject to the terms and conditions stated on the Usage Policy Statement on **www.myreportlinks.com.**
A password may be required to access the Report Links that back up this book. The password is found on the bottom of page 4 of this book.
Any comments or suggestions can be sent by e-mail to comments@myreportlinks.com or to the address on the back cover.

♻ Enslow Publishers, Inc., is committed to printing our books on recycled paper. The paper in every book contains 10% to 30% post-consumer waste (PCW). The cover board on the outside of each book contains 100% PCW. Our goal is to do our part to help young people and the environment too!

Photo Credits: AccessExcellence.org, p. 28; The Burndy Library, Dibner Institute for the History of Science and Technology, pp. 44, 64, 74, 104; DiscoverMagazine.com, p. 96; © Enslow, pp. 10, 24; FDA.gov, pp. 76, 111; The French Government Tourist Office, p. 70; History in Focus, p. 19; HistoryofBiologyandMedicine.com, p. 68; HowStuffWorks.com, p. 58; Infectious Disease Society of America, p. 80; The Institute for Animal Health, p. 54; KeepKidsHealthy.com, p. 94; Library of Congress, p. 5; Library of Congress Prints and Photographs Division, p. 110; Modern Drug Discovery, p. 88; Modern History Sourcebook/Fordham University, p. 62; Nancy Tomes/ Virginia Tech, p. 86; National Library of Medicine, pp. 38, 52, 59, 98, 100, 102, 112; NNDB.com, p. 50; NobelPrize.org, p. 47; The Pasteur Galaxy/php.pasteur.net, p. 115; PasteurFoundation.org, p. 39; PBS, pp. 15, 18; Photos.com, pp. 30, 85; Rabies.com, p. 117; R.B. Pearson/http://www.whale.to/a/b/pearson.html, p. 72; The Royal Society, p. 46; Shutterstock, pp. 8, 12, 26, 42, 56, 78, 108; Sudhir Cherukulappurath, p. 34; Time.com, pp. 92, 103; Time & Life Pictures/Getty Images, p. 82, 98; Timelinescience.org, p. 21; The University of Louisville, p. 60; The University of Virginia, p. 16; The University of Washington, p. 106; Wellcome Library, p. 48; WorldWideSchool.org, p. 23.

Cover Photo: (Pasteur) Library of Congress Prints and Photographs Division; (microscope) The Burndy Library, Dibner Institute for the History of Science and Technology

Contents

MyReportLinks.com Books
Great Books, Great Links, Great for Research!

The Internet sites featured in this book can save you hours of research time. These Internet sites—we call them **"Report Links"**—are constantly changing, but we keep them up to date on our Web site.

When you see this "Approved Web Site" logo, you will know that we are directing you to a great Internet site that will help you with your research.

Give it a try! Type http://www.myreportlinks.com into your browser, click on the series title and enter the password, then click on the book title, and scroll down to the Report Links listed for this book.

The Report Links will bring you to great source documents, photographs, and illustrations. MyReportLinks.com Books save you time, feature Report Links that are kept up to date, and make report writing easier than ever! A complete listing of the Report Links can be found on pages 120–121 at the back of the book.

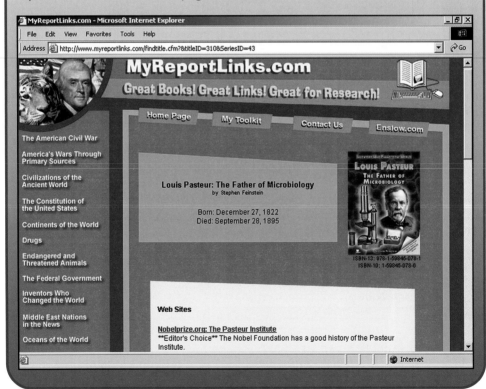

Please see "To Our Readers" on the copyright page for important information about this book, the MyReportLinks.com Web site, and the Report Links that back up this book.

Please enter **LPM1332** if asked for a password.

In the field of observation, chance favors only the prepared mind.

—Louis Pasteur

Important Dates

1822—Louis Pasteur is born on December 27 in Dole, France.

1827—The Pasteur family moves to Arbois.

1838—Pasteur and his friend Jules Vercel leave for Paris; Pasteur returns home a month later.

1839—Graduates from the College d'Arbois.

1840—Graduates from the royal college of Franche-Comté at Besançon.

1841—Fails the exam for his bachelor of science degree.

1842—Retakes and passes the exam and is awarded a bachelor of science degree.

1844—Enters the École Normale Supérieure.

1845—Graduates from the École Normale Supérieure.

1848—Appointed professor of chemistry at the University of Strasbourg.

1849—Marries Marie Laurent on May 29.

1853—The Society of Pharmacy awards Pasteur a 1,500-franc prize for turning tartaric acid into racemic acid.

1854—Appointed professor of chemistry and dean of the Faculty of Sciences at the University of Lille.

1857—Presents a paper on lactic fermentation; he is appointed administrator and director of scientific studies at the École Normale Supérieure.

1862—Elected to the French National Academy of Sciences.

1863—Begins study of wine and why it spoils.

1864—The Academy of Sciences awards Pasteur a 2,500-franc prize for proving that spontaneous generation does not exist.

1865—Begins his research on the diseases of the silkworm.

1868—Suffers a stroke on October 19.

1870—Publishes his book *Studies on the Diseases of the Silkworm.*

1873—Admitted as an associate member of the Academy of Medicine; develops germ theory of disease.

1877—Begins his research on anthrax.

1878—Publishes *The Theory of Germs and Its Applications to Medicine and Surgery.*

1880—Creates a vaccine for chicken cholera.

1881—Conducts a successful anthrax vaccination experiment at Pouilly le Fort.

1884—Produces his first vaccine for rabies.

1885—Vaccinates nine-year-old Joseph Meister against rabies.

1888—The Pasteur Institute opens in Paris on November 14.

1895—Louis Pasteur dies on September 28.

INCIDENT AT ARBOIS

When Louis Pasteur was a young boy, he and his family lived in Arbois, a small French village about 250 miles southeast of Paris. In October 1831, when Louis was nine years old, a wolf wandered out of the nearby woods and bit many town residents. The wolf had rabies, a very serious disease that can kill anyone who contracts it.

Medicine in the nineteenth century was very primitive and doctors had no idea what caused many diseases, including rabies. They certainly did not know how best to treat it. They had no idea that rabies was a disease caused by a virus, a tiny organism that can only be seen through a powerful microscope. If an infected animal, in this case the wolf, bites a human, rabies can be transmitted from the animal to the human. In 1831, rabies often killed anyone who was unlucky enough to be infected with it.

When Pasteur was just a child, people knew almost nothing about things like viruses and

CHAPTER

1

how to protect against them. In those days, the accepted treatment for someone who had rabies was to try to kill the virus by burning the victims' bites with a red-hot iron. This often worked—but not always—and it was incredibly painful.

Still, it was the best treatment available at the time and it was better than nothing.

In Arbois, there was a blacksmith shop close to the Pasteur home. Louis watched as the people who had been bitten by the wolf lined up outside, waiting for their turn to have the disease burned from their body. As the blacksmith burned each victim's bites with a piece of red-hot metal, Louis covered his ears with his hands, trying to block out the sound of their screams. But despite the drastic treatment, it has been reported that eight of Pasteur's neighbors died as a result of having been bitten by that wolf.

It is hard to imagine that anyone could ever forget witnessing another person allow himself be burned by hot metal and it seems reasonable to assume that Louis never forgot. But whether or not that scene from his childhood motivated Louis to become a scientist

Pasteur and his family lived in the small village of Arbois, approximately 250 miles southeast of Paris.

is not important. What does matter is that Louis Pasteur would one day develop the world's first successful vaccine to treat rabies, meaning that horrible scenes like the one he witnessed that day in Arbois would never have to be repeated.

Pasteur's discovery of the rabies vaccine was certainly one of his greatest achievements and one of the reasons why he is called the father of microbiology, the science of microscopic organisms. But it is truly a measure of Pasteur's greatness that the rabies vaccine was merely one of the many contributions he made to the fields of science and medicine—and why he is widely recognized as one of the world's greatest inventors.

Early Beliefs About Disease

Before the 1800s, doctors had no idea that diseases were caused by microscopic viruses, bacteria and other disease-causing pathogens. Thousands of years ago, people believed that disease was brought on by the gods as a form of punishment. Still others believed that disease resulted from magic performed by one's enemies. And there were even those who believed that an illness indicated the presence of evil spirits. Deadly epidemics might be blamed on things as simple as air, or water.

Obviously, healers in ancient societies did not have the benefit of advanced scientific knowledge or technologies to help them treat disease. Even still, every once in a while, they stumbled on treatments that worked. For example, opium, a powerful drug that is made from seeds of the poppy plant, was discovered to be a

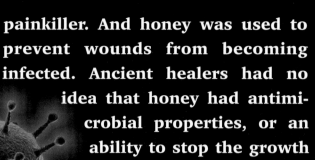

CHAPTER

2

painkiller. And honey was used to prevent wounds from becoming infected. Ancient healers had no idea that honey had antimicrobial properties, or an ability to stop the growth or spread of disease. But they could see that it worked. In fact, healers in many cultures had extensive knowledge of herbs and understood that they could be used as specific remedies for certain diseases or symptoms.

As long ago as 500 B.C., doctors in India performed eye surgery. In the process, they discovered that patients healed better after surgery if cotton pads soaked with fat were placed over their eyes. These doctors knew nothing about bacteria or that the fat formed a barrier that prevented bacteria from entering the eyes while they healed.[1]

In still other ancient societies, healers treated patients using a practice known as trephination, which involved drilling a hole in the patient's skull. It was believed that this procedure released the demons causing the patient's disease. Amazingly, some patients actually survived the treatment—we know this because archaeologists studying ancient human remains have identified instances where regrowth of the skull bone is evident.

⊛ THE "FATHER OF MEDICINE"

The ancient Greek physician Hippocrates was born on the island of Kos in Greece about 460 B.C. He is believed to be the first physician to challenge the then-dominant view that disease was caused by evil spirits or by the gods as a form of punishment. Instead, Hippocrates believed that disease had a physical cause and could be explained, and that things like diet and living habits, even the environment in which one lived, played a role in disease. He reasoned that there must be certain things in the atmosphere, soil, water, and food that made people more or less likely to get a particular disease. This idea is reflected in a section of the Hippocratic writings called "Air, Water and Places."

Hippocrates based his medical practice on observation and on the study of the human body. He focused his treatment on patient care and prognosis, or accurately describing symptoms. But Hippocrates knew nothing about microorganisms, or microbes, and could not determine the precise cause of a particular disease. So Hippocratic medicine was weak on diagnosis. Nevertheless, by relying on the natural healing processes of rest, a good diet, fresh air, and cleanliness, Hippocrates treated many patients successfully. In time, he came to be regarded as the greatest physician of his time.

⊜A "Humorous" Concept of Disease

Among his many accomplishments in medicine, Hippocrates developed an Oath of Medical Ethics, or the Hippocratic Oath, which defines standards

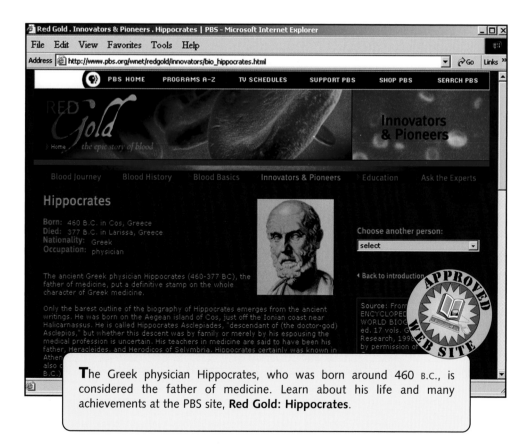

The Greek physician Hippocrates, who was born around 460 B.C., is considered the father of medicine. Learn about his life and many achievements at the PBS site, **Red Gold: Hippocrates**.

of good medical practice. The oath is still taken by doctors today when they graduate from medical school and begin their career. Despite that direct connection, the practice of medicine in Hippocrates' time is almost unrecognizable when it is compared to what we know today as modern medicine.

Hippocrates believed that the body was composed of four liquids or "humors": black bile, yellow bile, blood, and phlegm. These fluids were supposedly equal in proportion within the body. When the four humors were unbalanced, a person would become sick and he or she would remain sick until the balance was restored.

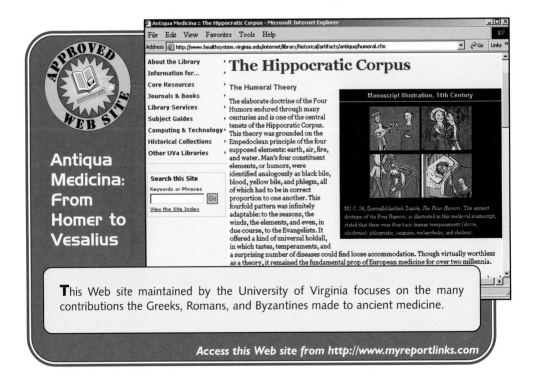

APPROVED WEB SITE

Antiqua Medicina: From Homer to Vesalius

The Hippocrates Corpus

The Humoral Theory

The elaborate doctrine of the Four Humors endured through many centuries and is one of the central tenets of the Hippocratic Corpus. This theory was grounded on the Empedoclean principle of the four supposed elements: earth, air, fire, and water. Man's four constituent elements, or humors, were identified analogously as black bile, blood, yellow bile, and phlegm, all of which had to be in correct proportion to one another. This fourfold pattern was infinitely adaptable: to the seasons, the winds, the elements, and even, in due course, to the Evangelists. It offered a kind of universal holdall, in which tastes, temperaments, and a surprising number of diseases could find loose accommodation. Though virtually worthless as a theory, it remained the fundamental prop of European medicine for over two millennia.

Manuscript Illustration, 14th Century

MS C. 54, Zentralbibliothek Zurich, *The Four Humors*. The ancient doctrine of the Four Humors, as illustrated in this medieval manuscript, stated that there were four basic human temperaments (above, clockwise): phlegmatic, sanguine, melancholic, and choleric.

This Web site maintained by the University of Virginia focuses on the many contributions the Greeks, Romans, and Byzantines made to ancient medicine.

Access this Web site from http://www.myreportlinks.com

Hippocrates believed the body had the power to rebalance the four humors and heal itself. He devised treatments to help that process. The four humors corresponded to what the Greeks believed to be the four elements of matter: earth, water, air, and fire. The Greeks also believed in four primary qualities: dry, hot, wet, and cold. So when a person developed a fever, it was believed the illness was a result of too much yellow bile. A cold, wet bath was prescribed. The Greeks thought the common cold was caused by an increase in cold, wet phlegm, so the patient was told to drink wine and stay in bed wrapped in blankets. This would lead to an increase in the patient's hot, dry yellow bile.

Hippocrates' doctrine of the four humors remained the basic concept of human health and disease in Europe for more than two thousand years. And because the four humors could be made to explain just about any medical situation or illness, their acceptance discouraged fresh analytical thinking.

RECONSIDERING CONTAGION

Despite the fact that most people believed that disease was the result of divine or supernatural forces, it had occurred to some people that certain diseases could be contagious. That is, they could be spread by physical contact, the sharing of clothing or other objects, and even by tiny organisms

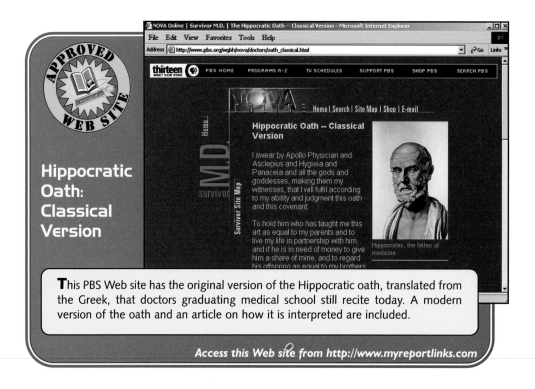

Hippocratic
Oath:
Classical
Version

NOVA Online | Survivor M.D. | The Hippocratic Oath -- Classical Version - Microsoft Internet Explorer

File Edit View Favorites Tools Help

Address http://www.pbs.org/wgbh/nova/doctors/oath_classical.html

thirteen PBS HOME   PROGRAMS A-Z   TV SCHEDULES   SUPPORT PBS   SHOP PBS   SEARCH PBS

NOVA   Home | Search | Site Map | Shop | E-mail

Hippocratic Oath -- Classical Version

I swear by Apollo Physician and Asclepius and Hygieia and Panaceia and all the gods and goddesses, making them my witnesses, that I will fulfil according to my ability and judgment this oath and this covenant:

To hold him who has taught me this art as equal to my parents and to live my life in partnership with him, and if he is in need of money to give him a share of mine, and to regard his offspring as equal to my brothers

Hippocrates, the father of medicine

This PBS Web site has the original version of the Hippocratic oath, translated from the Greek, that doctors graduating medical school still recite today. A modern version of the oath and an article on how it is interpreted are included.

Access this Web site from http://www.myreportlinks.com

in the air. How else, they reasoned, could one explain epidemics of the plague, cholera, or influenza that made so many people sick?

As early as the first century B.C., Marcus Terentius Varro, a Roman scholar, expressed the idea that disease was caused by invisible living things—*animalia minuta*—taken into the body with food or breathed in with air.[2] Varro went so far as to write that "the air in these [swamps] swarms with tiny and invisible animals which, sucked in by the mouth, penetrate into the body, where they engender [produce] diseases."[3] However, Varro had no evidence to support his theory, so it was largely ignored.

During the fourteenth century, the bubonic plague, one of the most far-reaching epidemics of all time, swept through Europe. Known as the Black Death because of the purplish or black spots on the skin of its victims, the plague killed nearly 25 million people—about one third of Europe's population—and millions more in Asia and North Africa. Europeans, terrified of the disease and not understanding what caused it, looked for and found a scapegoat—Europe's Jews.

Rumors quickly spread that the Jews in many towns had poisoned the wells and were to blame for the plague. As a result, thousands of Jews throughout Europe were murdered, many burned

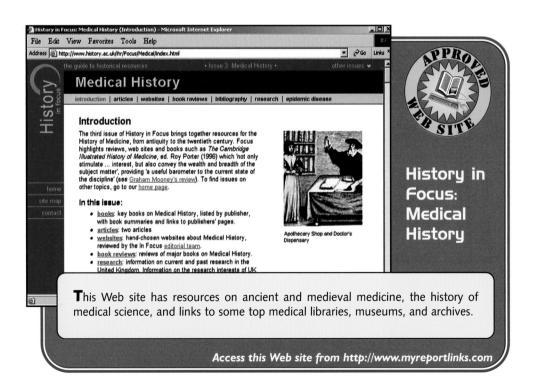

This Web site has resources on ancient and medieval medicine, the history of medical science, and links to some top medical libraries, museums, and archives.

Access this Web site from http://www.myreportlinks.com

alive. The bubonic plague returned to Europe several more times in the fourteenth and in the fifteenth centuries.

In the late fifteenth and early sixteenth centuries, an epidemic of syphilis, a sexual disease, spread through Europe. In an effort to help explain how a disease could affect such large numbers of people, the concept of contagion resurfaced. In 1546, the Italian physician Girolamo Fracastoro proposed that diseases can be transmitted by a living agent, or a *contagium vivum*.[4] These tiny particles, spores or seeds of contagion, could transmit infection by direct or indirect contact.

Fracastoro could not identify the true physical nature of his disease-bearing living germs. And because he could not support his ideas with scientific evidence, he could not convince fellow doctors of their merit. Without evidence that proved his theory, people were more inclined to believe in the miasma theory, which stated that diseased and decaying bodies altered the chemical quality of the atmosphere. The idea that infectious diseases were of microbial origin would have to wait about three hundred years—or until Louis Pasteur proposed his germ theory of disease.

It's a Small World

In 1590, Zacharias Janssen and his father, Hans, Dutch eyeglass makers, began experimenting with

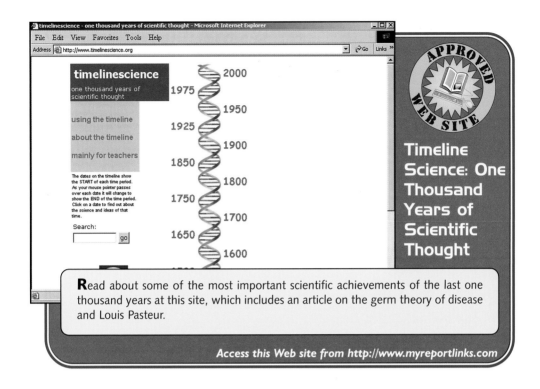

timelinescience

one thousand years of
scientific thought

using the timeline

about the timeline

mainly for teachers

The dates on the timeline show
the START of each time period.
As your mouse pointer passes
over each date it will change to
show the END of the time period.
Click on a date to find out about
the science and ideas of that
time.

Search:

[   ] go

2000
1975
1950
1925
1900
1850
1800
1750
1700
1650
1600

Timeline Science: One Thousand Years of Scientific Thought

Read about some of the most important scientific achievements of the last one thousand years at this site, which includes an article on the germ theory of disease and Louis Pasteur.

Access this Web site from http://www.myreportlinks.com

lenses. They noticed that when they put several lenses in a tube, the object at the other end of the tube seemed much larger. The magnification power of their lenses was much greater than that of a simple magnifying glass. Because it used two-or-more lenses, their discovery came to be known as a compound microscope.

In 1646, Athanasius Kircher, a German scholar, began using a microscope to study the blood of plague victims. In 1658, he observed the presence of a swarming mass of animalcula, or tiny animals in the blood. He concluded that the plague was caused by infectious microorganisms.[5] Although Kircher was correct, he most likely had seen red or white blood cells rather than *Yersinia pestis,* the bacterium that caused the plague.

Meanwhile in Holland, Anthoni van Leeuwenhoek had become interested in lenses while working with magnifying glasses in a dry-goods store. Van Leeuwenhoek used the magnifying glass to count threads in woven cloth. Van Leeuwenhoek learned how to make his own lenses, grinding and polishing small lenses with great curvatures. His single lenses were more round and produced a great magnification. With his microscope, van Leeuwenhoek was able to see things that no human had ever seen before, such as bacteria and yeast.

The seventeenth-century English scientist Robert Hooke was another who experimented with microscopes. He examined tiny animals, plants, and even snowflakes. He observed cells while looking at a sliver of cork. Though these developments were interesting, Kircher's, van Leeuwenhoek's, and Hooke's observations did not make a lasting impression, because their discoveries were thought to be accidental. The supposed infectious agents, invisible to the naked eye, simply did not fit the accepted medical ideas of the time.

➔ IDEAS ABOUT DISEASE IN THE EARLY 1800s

By the early nineteenth century, understanding of diseases and what caused them had not improved much since the time of Hippocrates. There were a few scientists who believed that bacteria and other microorganisms somehow caused disease, but most scientists still scoffed at the notion. They refused to believe that something so tiny could cause terrible sickness. The concept of contagion was still hotly debated.

Since there was as yet no real understanding of the true nature of diseases and their causes, effective treatments were often lacking. In the early 1800s, hundreds of medicines and other types of remedies existed for every type of sickness, but few of them were really effective. For the most part, whether or not a medicine worked was the result of pure chance. Certainly, no one truly

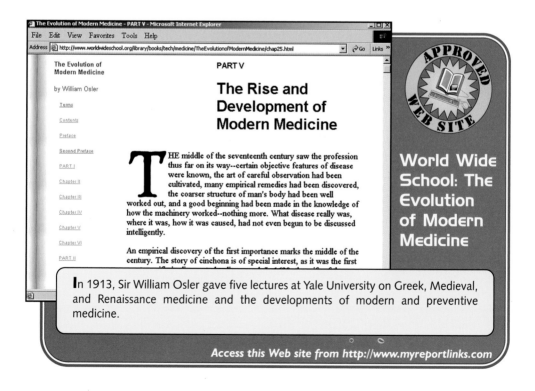

In 1913, Sir William Osler gave five lectures at Yale University on Greek, Medieval, and Renaissance medicine and the developments of modern and preventive medicine.

Access this Web site from http://www.myreportlinks.com

Buste de Paul Dubois.

Léveillé, sculpsit.

▲ Like all great scientists and inventors, Pasteur relied on and improved upon the work and study of those who came before him.

understood why some medicines worked while others did not.

In fact, at the time, most scientists still believed in the theory of spontaneous generation. According to this widely held belief, living things can spring from other living or even nonliving things—or even from the air. For example, maggots that appeared in rotting meat and then turned into flies came from the meat.

By the 1800s, scientists had altered their thinking slightly, claiming that spontaneous generation did not apply to animals one could actually see; still, the argument went, microbes were certainly spontaneously generated. The theory of spontaneous generation persisted until 1864, when Louis Pasteur conducted experiments that disproved it.

THE EARLY YEARS

Louis Pasteur was born at home on December 27, 1822, in the small town of Dole in eastern France. Louis's father, Jean-Joseph, was a tanner—he took the hides of animals and treated them so that they could be made into shoes and other items. His tannery was in the backyard, where he prepared the leather by scraping, beating, and cleansing hides with oil or grease.

Louis was the second son born to Jean-Joseph and his wife Jeanne, (the Pasteurs' first son had died six years earlier when he was just a few months old). Louis's older sister Virginie was born in 1818. Louis also had two younger sisters, Josephine, born in 1825, and Emilie, who was born in 1826.

The year Emilie was born, the family moved to the nearby town of Marnoz, where they lived with Jeanne Pasteur's mother. Jean-Joseph tried to establish a tanning business, but he was unsuccessful. So in 1827, when Louis was five years old,

the Pasteur family moved again, this time to Arbois, a nearby town that sat at the foot of the Jura Mountains. Arbois, surrounded by vineyards, was known for its fine wines. Jean-Joseph was able to acquire an existing tannery there.

CHAPTER

3

The Pasteur family lived in a stone house on the banks of the Cuisance River. The tannery workshop was located in the basement, and the family lived upstairs. Louis had a loving family and a happy childhood. His mother focused a lot of attention on her three daughters, but she never hesitated to express her affection for her son.

Louis enjoyed playing with his friends. In the summer, they swam and fished in the river. Often they played in the yard outside the tannery, where they would find scraps of leather and make slingshots. During the grape harvest in the fall, there were always games for the children. In the winter, Louis and his friends would go sledding or strap on wooden shoes and slide across the frozen river.

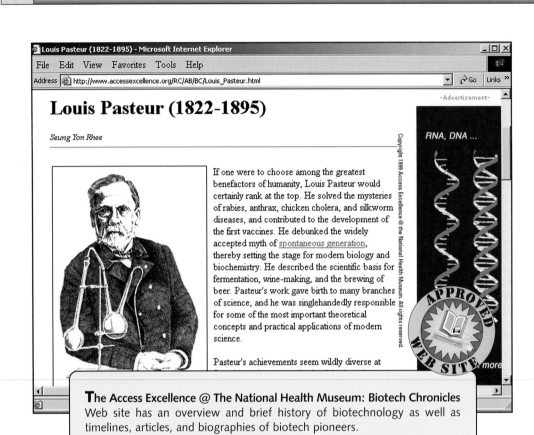

Louis Pasteur (1822-1895) - Microsoft Internet Explorer

File   Edit   View   Favorites   Tools   Help

Address   http://www.accessexcellence.org/RC/AB/BC/Louis_Pasteur.html

-Advertisement-

Louis Pasteur (1822-1895)

Seung Yon Rhee

If one were to choose among the greatest benefactors of humanity, Louis Pasteur would certainly rank at the top. He solved the mysteries of rabies, anthrax, chicken cholera, and silkworm diseases, and contributed to the development of the first vaccines. He debunked the widely accepted myth of spontaneous generation, thereby setting the stage for modern biology and biochemistry. He described the scientific basis for fermentation, wine-making, and the brewing of beer. Pasteur's work gave birth to many branches of science, and he was singlehandedly responsible for some of the most important theoretical concepts and practical applications of modern science.

Pasteur's achievements seem wildly diverse at

RNA, DNA ...

APPROVED WEB SITE

The Access Excellence @ The National Health Museum: Biotech Chronicles Web site has an overview and brief history of biotechnology as well as timelines, articles, and biographies of biotech pioneers.

JEAN-JOSEPH: WAR HERO

Jean-Joseph Pasteur worked hard to support his family. He worked long hours in his tannery six days a week, and the work was physically exhausting. But he always found time to go for long walks on Sundays with his only son. The two would often follow the road from Arbois to Besançon, which ran through the hilly vine-yards. Jean-Joseph wore an old coat he'd gotten when he was in the army. Attached to the lapel of that coat was his red ribbon of the Legion of Honor.

On those walks, Jean-Joseph would tell Louis about his experiences as a soldier in the Napoleonic Wars, which France fought between 1799 and 1815. Jean-Joseph looked back on those days as the most intense and exciting time of his life. He felt it had been a great honor to serve his emperor, Napoléon I, and fight in Spain. For his service, Jean-Joseph had been made a chevalier, or knight, of the Legion of Honor. He impressed on Louis the importance of military honor, justice, and duty in the service of his country and his emperor.

⇒ VIVE LA FRANCE

Jean-Joseph excelled in the army and eventually he became a sergeant. In the last battle in which he was involved, only 284 soldiers from a regiment of 8,000 survived. The emperor himself awarded the Sword of Honor to Jean-Joseph for his bravery. When Napoléon was defeated and overthrown in 1815, Jean-Joseph refused to surrender his sword. He proudly hung it on the wall in his home, right next to a portrait of the emperor.

Louis came to realize that his father viewed tannery work as tedious and dirty. Jean-Joseph made it clear to his son that he did not want him

Pasteur's father, Jean-Joseph, was a soldier in the Napoleonic Wars and a patriotic Frenchman. Here Emperor Napoléon, who personally awarded the Sword of Honor to Jean-Joseph, leads his troops into battle in 1814.

to follow in his footsteps. Instead, he expected Louis to become a teacher at the College d'Arbois, a local secondary school, like an American high school. To make sure that Louis would achieve the goal he had set for him, Jean-Joseph became deeply involved in his education. He became his son's private tutor, first teaching Louis the alphabet and then how to read. Louis would later say about his father, "In teaching me to read, you made sure that I learned about the greatness of France."[1]

→ DEDICATED FAMILY MAN

According to a neighbor of the Pasteurs, Jean-Joseph was firm but fair—and devoted to his family. "The father exercised absolute yet wise and reasoned authority over his entire family; but there was nothing tyrannical about his will, for it was always tempered by love and kindness."[2]

Many years later, in 1883, a plaque was placed at the house in which Louis was born in Dole. At the ceremony, Pasteur thanked his parents for their love and support, for helping to make his many scientific achievements possible.

> Your enthusiasm, my brave mother, you bequeathed to me. And you, my dear father, you showed me what patience can accomplish when the task is long. It is to you that I owe my tenacity in carrying out the work that needs to be done from day to day.[3]

⇒ SCHOOL DAYS

In 1831, Louis entered first grade at the local one-room school. The teacher, who often divided the class into smaller groups, would choose a student in each group to help with the lessons. During his first few years at school, Louis was not an outstanding student, but he was occasionally chosen to be a group leader. Louis would always remember his first-grade teacher, Mr. Renaud, for giving him a profound respect for learning.

As the years went by, Louis's academic work improved greatly. He had begun to show enthusiasm for learning, and he worked hard. A family friend, Mr. Romanet, principal of the College d'Arbois, recognized Louis's ability. He suggested to Jean-Joseph that Louis consider becoming a student at the École Normale Supérieure, one of the most prestigious universities in Paris. Romanet said, however, that in order to be admitted to that university, Louis would first have to go to a secondary school in Paris.

In October 1838, Louis and his friend Jules Vercel traveled to Paris. There they enrolled in the College Saint-Louis, a private preparatory school. Louis had never been away from home before and he became terribly homesick. He hated having to wear the school uniform. He was so sad and distracted by his strange surroundings and all of the new people around him that he could not keep

In 1883, French authorities placed a plaque at Pasteur's birthplace in Dole. It reads "Here was born Louis Pasteur, 27 December 1822."

his mind on his studies. Louis expressed his unhappiness in his letters home. And he told his friend Jules, "If I could only smell the odor of the tannery, I am sure I would feel much better."[4] In mid-November, Jean-Joseph went to Paris and brought his son home. Louis returned to school at the College d'Arbois.

→Finding Peace in Painting

Louis's confidence had been shaken by his experience in Paris. He now put a lot of his time and energy into art. He liked to paint portraits of the important people in his life, especially his mother and father. His approach was to try to make the portraits as realistic as he could. He focused on every detail, painting with great precision.

Even as a young child, Louis had liked to draw. His mother had encouraged him, buying art supplies. His teachers had recognized his artistic ability and praised his drawings. But Jean-Joseph was not happy; art was a fine hobby, but it was not to be taken seriously as a profession. Jean-Joseph still wanted his son to become a teacher.

According to some people, Louis might have become a great painter had he focused on art. In a letter to a friend, Finnish artist Albert Edelfeldt, who painted a famous portrait of Pasteur in his laboratory in 1887, wrote "I am certain that had

M. Pasteur selected art instead of science, France would count today one more able painter. . . ."[5]

Artistic ability notwithstanding, before long, Louis came around to his father's way of thinking about his future. And Romanet, at the College d'Arbois, continued to compliment Louis on his academic work, hoping to restore the young man's confidence in the process. Clearly, the strategy worked, because Louis once more threw himself into his studies.

⮕ DIFFICULT EXAMINATIONS

In the spring of 1839, Louis Pasteur graduated from the College d'Arbois. But he was not yet ready to return to Paris. Instead, he decided to continue his education at the royal college of Franche-Comté in the city of Besançon, the district capital. There, Louis studied philosophy, history, Latin, Greek, mathematics, and science. He hated math, having no use for its abstract concepts. He did, however, like his science classes. And he continued to draw portraits of the people around him.

Pasteur was enthusiastic about his studies—so much so that he wrote letters of advice to his sisters, hoping his own enthusiasm would inspire them to work hard. "Work . . . may at first cause disgust and boredom," he wrote, "but one who has become used to work can no longer live without it

Offert par Mr Deschiens.

Strasbourg 6 juillet 1850

L. Pasteur

▲ *This scholarly pose not withstanding, Pasteur's early academic experience was mixed—he failed the exam for his bachelor's degree the first time he took it.*

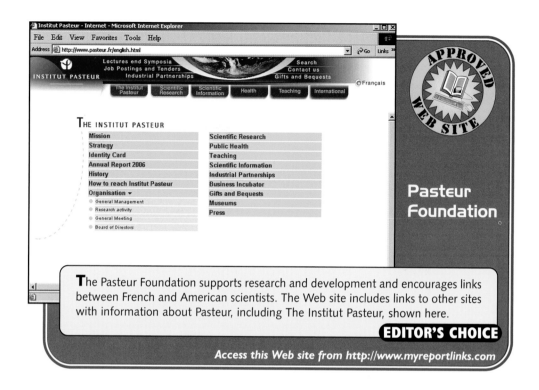

The Pasteur Foundation supports research and development and encourages links between French and American scientists. The Web site includes links to other sites with information about Pasteur, including The Institut Pasteur, shown here.

EDITOR'S CHOICE

Access this Web site from http://www.myreportlinks.com

. . . with knowledge one is happy, with knowledge one rises above others."[6] In another letter, he said, ". . . Action and Work usually follow Will, and almost always Work is accompanied by Success. These three things, Work, Will and Success, fill human existence. Will opens the door to success both brilliant and happy; Work passes these doors, and at the end of the journey Success comes to crown one's efforts."[7] He might not have known it at the time, but in these letters, Pasteur was clearly formulating his own philosophy of life—a philosophy that would propel him to great scientific achievements.

→Jobs Well Done

Pasteur's hard work paid off and he graduated in 1840. Still, his grades were adequate, not outstanding and with the exception of science, his work was not strong enough to gain him admission to the École Normale Supérieure in Paris. He decided instead to study for another year at Besançon to earn a bachelor of science degree.

At the end of the year, Pasteur took the final exams for the bachelor's degree. These exams were extremely difficult and many students who took them failed. So did Louis. But unlike those who dropped out of school after failing, Louis was determined to try again. He went to Paris and enrolled once again in the College Saint-Louis, the same private preparatory school where he had been so unhappy in 1838. This time, Louis was ready to live away from home and he enjoyed being in Paris. It helped that a good friend of his, Charles Chappuis, was also studying in Paris. The two friends spent many enjoyable hours exploring Paris together. Louis was happy and his studies went well.

While in Paris, Pasteur attended lectures at the Sorbonne by the famous chemist Jean-Baptiste Dumas. One of the founders of organic chemistry, Dumas was devoted to the study of the chemical changes associated with living processes. In his lectures, he explained the work he had done in organic chemistry. Louis was very inspired by Dumas's lectures and he became fascinated with chemistry and how it could be applied to everyday life.

In 1842, Louis once again took the exams for his bachelor of science degree. This time, he passed easily. And in 1843, he took the entrance exams for the École Normale Supérieure. He passed these as well and was admitted to the science department of the École Normale.

A Scientist Is Born

In October 1843, Louis Pasteur began studying physics and chemistry at the École Normale. His life as a student consisted of twelve-hour days of study, lectures, and laboratory work. He became so involved in his work that he had very little time for anything else. Indeed, his father, Jean-Joseph, began to worry about his son's almost obsessive devotion to his work. At one point, he became so alarmed that he wrote to Louis's friend Charles, urging him to drag Louis out of the laboratory and on walks around Paris.

Pasteur's First Experiment

Pasteur's science professors had often remarked on the difficulty of obtaining natural phosphorus, an essential element for all living cells. Not only was the procedure difficult, it was time-consuming and dangerous as well. Pasteur took these warnings as a challenge—if he could successfully produce phosphorus, he would demonstrate the validity of a lesson taught in class. Moreover, he would demonstrate his

Louis got some animal bones from a nearby butcher shop. He then reduced the bones to ashes and added sulfuric acid. Filtering the mixture produced a kind of heavy syrup. When this was heated, it gave off a vapor of phosphorus that condensed in water. In the end, Pasteur produced a few grams of phosphorus. Suddenly, broad new horizon opened up before his eyes ar Pasteur saw his life in a new light—he no long wanted to become a teacher. He now kne he wanted to be a scientist making his ow discoveries.

→ EXPERIMENTS IN CRYSTALLOGRAPHY

As Pasteur became more deeply involve in his science studies, he grew more an more excited about his possible future a a scientist. What interested him most wa the challenge of finding solutions to que tions that still puzzled the world's leadin scientists.

In 1845, Pasteur passed his final examina tions at the École and earned his teachin certificate. The Ministry of Education gave hir an assignment to teach physics at a secondar school in a small town a position that migl

Developed more than 230 years earlier, the microscope played a huge role in the life and career of Louis Pasteur. Shown here, one of the scientist's many microscopes.

have satisfied Pasteur in the past. Now, it no longer interested him. He wanted to spend his time learning new things in the laboratory. He was intent on becoming a scientist.

Pasteur's chemistry professor at the École was Antoine Jérôme Balard, a young scientist who, in 1826, had discovered the element bromine when he was just twenty-four years old. Pasteur pleaded with Balard to allow him to continue at the École to study for his doctoral degree. Balard, who saw that Pasteur was a very promising science student, convinced the Ministry of Education that his talents would be wasted in a small village in the middle of nowhere.

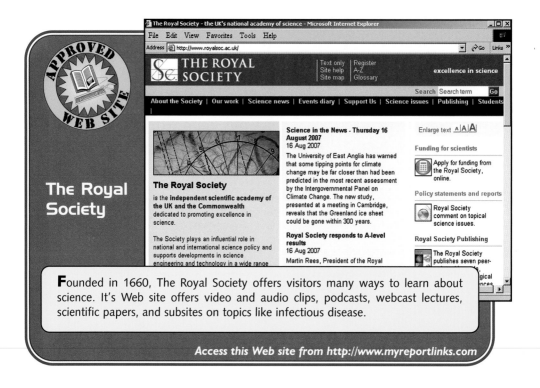

The Royal Society

Founded in 1660, The Royal Society offers visitors many ways to learn about science. It's Web site offers video and audio clips, podcasts, webcast lectures, scientific papers, and subsites on topics like infectious disease.

Access this Web site from http://www.myreportlinks.com

Balard took on Pasteur as his laboratory assistant. At this time in his life, Balard was more interested in the work of other scientists than he was in conducting his own experiments. As a result, he encouraged Pasteur to do independent research and experimentation. Pasteur could not have been happier, for now he had a perfect opportunity to learn and make discoveries.

One of Pasteur's teachers at the École, Gabriel Delafosse, had published a study on the geometrical, physical, and chemical properties of crystals. Crystals are regularly shaped objects that many substances form when they harden. For example, when water vapor freezes, it hardens into crystals that form snowflakes. This new branch of chemistry was known as crystallography, the science dealing with the structures of crystals.

Toward the end of 1846, a young chemist named Auguste Laurent came to work in Balard's laboratory. Influenced by Laurent, Pasteur became even more interested in crystals. He later wrote,

> . . . One day it happened that M. Laurent— studying, if I mistake not, some tungstate of soda—showed me, through the microscope, that this salt, apparently very pure, was evidently a mixture of three distinct kinds of crystals . . . I began to study carefully the formations of a

At the Nobel Foundation Web site, you can read a history of the Pasteur Institute and find information about some of the many medical breakthroughs it pioneered.

EDITOR'S CHOICE

Access this Web site from http://www.myreportlinks.com

very fine series of compounds, all very easily crystallized; tartaric acid and the tartrates.[1]

At the École, Pasteur read an article by the German crystallographer and chemist Eilhardt Mitscherlich. The article discussed the two different crystalline forms of tartaric acids and their respective salts, the tartrates and paratartrates. Tartaric acid was a common by-product of wine-making. It was used in the textile dye industry, by pharmacists and as an ingredient in baking powder. Paratartaric, or racemic acid, which also

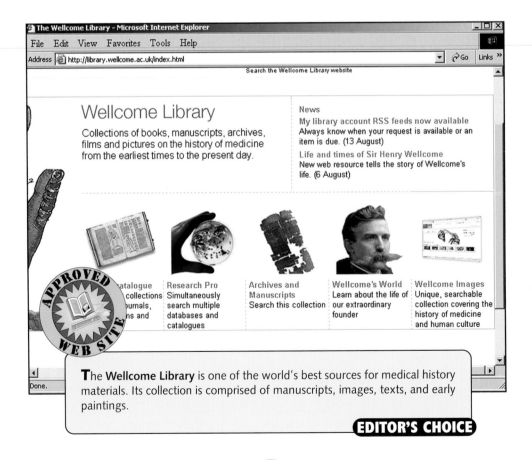

The **Wellcome Library** is one of the world's best sources for medical history materials. Its collection is comprised of manuscripts, images, texts, and early paintings.

EDITOR'S CHOICE

formed in the sediment of wine barrels, had the same chemical formula as tartaric acid.

According to Mitscherlich, the two forms of tartaric acids had the same chemical composition and the same crystal-shaped molecules with the same angles. But the tartaric acid was optically active and the racemic acid was optically inactive. This meant that when a beam of polarized light (meaning the beam of light vibrates) was passed through solutions of the two chemicals in a device called a polarimeter, the beam of polarized light would bend or rotate in the tartaric acid solution, but it would not bend in the racemic acid solution.

⟳ A Major Breakthrough

Pasteur wondered what was going on with the tartaric acids. The current scientific thinking on the subject did not seem to make sense. Pasteur believed there had to be some chemical difference between the two acids and that this would show up in the shape of the crystals. He began experimenting. He learned how to use a goniometer, an instrument that determines angles between crystal facets, or plane surfaces. He also learned how to use the polarimeter.

Hour after hour, Pasteur peered through his microscope and at the molecular crystals, or isomers, of the two acids. He observed, as had others, that both the tartaric and the racemic acid crystals were asymmetrical or not the same general shape. But then he noticed something that other scientists had overlooked. The crystals of both substances had a tiny sloping facet in one corner. But some of the racemic acid crystals had a tiny sloping facet, or flat surface, on the left side, while on others the facet was on the right.

Using a delicate needle and his microscope, Pasteur separated the left and right crystal shapes, forming two piles. He dissolved each group in water and then examined the solutions in a polarimeter. The solution of left-turning crystals rotated polarized light to the left, and the right-turning crystals rotated the polarized light to the

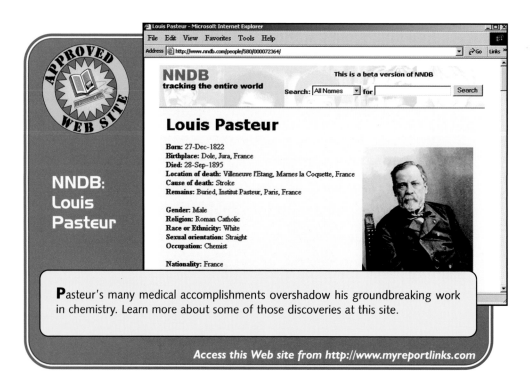

NNDB:
Louis
Pasteur

Pasteur's many medical accomplishments overshadow his groundbreaking work in chemistry. Learn more about some of those discoveries at this site.

Access this Web site from http://www.myreportlinks.com

right. When the solution consisted of equal amounts of left and right crystals, as in racemic acid, it did not rotate polarized light—in other words, the crystals canceled each other out.

Pasteur proved that some molecules could exist in mirror image, one right-handed and the other left-handed. He also showed that asymmetry is only present in organic compounds such as tartaric acid that had once been a living organism. Minerals such as quartz are not organic and they do not show the same kind of asymmetry. Pasteur's discovery of the asymmetry of organic molecules came to be known as molecular asymmetry. It would lead to a new branch of chemistry known as stereochemistry, which deals with the spatial arrangement of atoms and molecules and their relation to the properties of the compound.

⊜ CRYSTAL CLEAR

Pasteur's first major scientific discovery would have a tremendous impact on the course of scientific developments in chemistry and biology. In his biography of Pasteur, Patrice Debré, a French immunologist and physician, emphasizes the importance of Pasteur's achievements.

> Pasteur . . . gave the initial impulse to developments that allowed biology to achieve greater advances in a few decades than had been made in several centuries. . . .

▲ Pasteur, shown here in his lab at the École Normale Supérieure, made most of his great discoveries only after carefully conducting experiments in the lab.

Thanks to Pasteur, scientists . . . began to see that in living beings molecules constitute the functional units of every organism. . . . To understand their organization opens the approach to their specific function. . . .

In discovering the principles of molecular asymmetry, Pasteur had . . . unlocked the door to the whole of modern biology.[2]

⇒ PROFESSOR LOUIS PASTEUR

Balard, Pasteur's chemistry professor at the École, was very proud of his student. He brought Pasteur to the attention of Jean-Baptiste Biot, the famous French physicist. Biot had invented the polarimeter, used it in experiments with organic compounds, and had discovered those compounds' effect on polarized light beams. When Pasteur repeated his experiments in front of Biot, the physicist was very impressed—so much so that he became Pasteur's mentor.

At the same time he was conducting his experiments in the laboratory, Pasteur also wrote two long papers, or theses, which were required for his doctoral degree. His professors approved his chemistry thesis and his physics thesis and on August 28, 1847, Pasteur received his doctor of science degree.

The following year, 1848, was difficult for Pasteur. While he continued to work in Balard's laboratory, events in Paris created a major

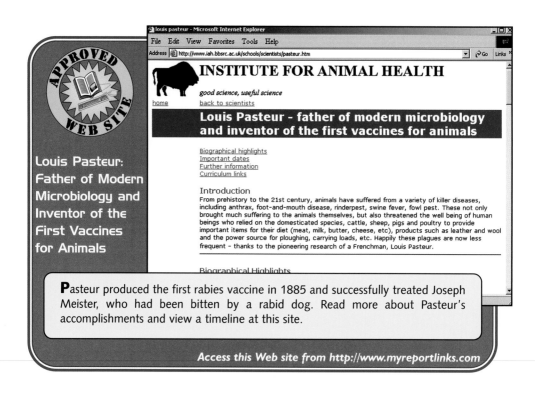

INSTITUTE FOR ANIMAL HEALTH

good science, useful science

home   back to scientists

Louis Pasteur - father of modern microbiology and inventor of the first vaccines for animals

Biographical highlights
Important dates
Further information
Curriculum links

Introduction

From prehistory to the 21st century, animals have suffered from a variety of killer diseases, including anthrax, foot-and-mouth disease, rinderpest, swine fever, fowl pest. These not only brought much suffering to the animals themselves, but also threatened the well being of human beings who relied on the domesticated species, cattle, sheep, pigs and poultry to provide important items for their diet (meat, milk, butter, cheese, etc), products such as leather and wool and the power source for ploughing, carrying loads, etc. Happily these plagues are now less frequent - thanks to the pioneering research of a Frenchman, Louis Pasteur.

Biographical Highlights

Louis Pasteur:
Father of Modern
Microbiology and
Inventor of the
First Vaccines
for Animals

Pasteur produced the first rabies vaccine in 1885 and successfully treated Joseph Meister, who had been bitten by a rabid dog. Read more about Pasteur's accomplishments and view a timeline at this site.

Access this Web site from http://www.myreportlinks.com

distraction. In February, a popular revolt began against the French king, Louis-Philippe. Mobs roamed the streets, and people were killed. Pasteur joined the National Guard, declaring he would fight for the cause of the Republic should it become necessary.

Meanwhile, in May 1848, Pasteur's mother, Jeanne, suffered a massive stroke. Pasteur rushed home to Arbois, but his mother had died by the time he arrived. After weeks spent consoling his family, Pasteur returned to Paris. Soon after, the Ministry of Education informed him that he would teach physics in a secondary school in the city of Dijon. Although this was the last thing he wanted to do, Pasteur had no choice but to accept the job. However, thanks to the help of Balard and Biot, within two months Pasteur was appointed professor of chemistry at the University of Strasbourg.

Pasteur was delighted. It had been a very difficult year, but things were looking up. By December, the political situation had calmed considerably. Louis-Napoléon, the nephew of Napoléon Bonaparte, was elected president, and the revolt was ending.

Pasteur arrived in Strasbourg, a large city in eastern France, on January 22, 1849, and moved in with an old friend, Pierre-Augustin Bertin. Almost immediately he began working at the University of Strasbourg.

FOCUSING ON FERMENTATION

Pasteur was excited to be in Strasbourg. The city was known for its various industries, and he hoped to find some practical uses there for his scientific discoveries. He was also pleased to discover that his new students were enthusiastic about his ideas and research. Pasteur had expected to continue working with crystals, but before a month had passed, a completely different subject came to occupy his thoughts.

LOVE AT FIRST SIGHT

Shortly after his arrival in Strasbourg, Pasteur was invited to the home of Charles Laurent, the head of the University of Strasbourg. There Pasteur met Marie, one of Laurent's daughters. On Pasteur's part at least, it must have been love at first sight, because he immediately wrote a letter asking Laurent for his daughter's hand in marriage. In the letter, Pasteur wrote about his family background and his devotion to scientific research. Regarding his personal qualities, he wrote, "All I possess is good health, a kind heart, and my position in the University."[1]

Laurent was slow to reply. At the end of March, Pasteur sent another letter. He also sent one to Marie, telling her, "I woke up suddenly with the thought that you did not love me and immediately started to cry. . . . My work no longer means anything to me. I who always used to wish in the evening that the night be shorter to come back the sooner to my studies."[2]

Eventually, to Pasteur's great relief and joy, Marie agreed to marry him. The wedding took place on May 29, 1849. From the beginning, Marie understood that science would always come first in Pasteur's life. According to Emile Roux, a man who knew the couple well, from the very first days of their shared life, "Mme. [Madame] Pasteur intuitively understood what kind of man she had married; she made it her task to keep the difficulties of daily life away from him . . . so that he might keep his mind free to pursue his research. Mme. Pasteur loved her husband so much

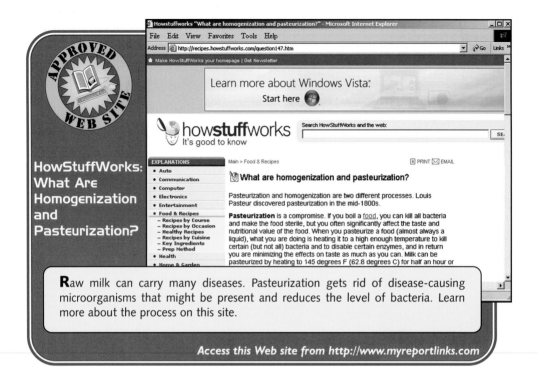

HowStuffWorks:
What Are
Homogenization
and
Pasteurization?

Raw milk can carry many diseases. Pasteurization gets rid of disease-causing microorganisms that might be present and reduces the level of bacteria. Learn more about the process on this site.

Access this Web site from http://www.myreportlinks.com

that she learned to understand his work. In the evening she would write down what he dictated and ask him to explain it. . . . Not only an incomparable mate, Mme. Pasteur was also his best collaborator."[3]

The Pasteurs' first child, a daughter named Jeanne, was born in April 1850. Four more children would follow in the coming years. The Pasteurs would have a long and happy marriage.

⊜ AN IMPORTANT PRIZE

At the University, Pasteur experimented with different chemicals to learn about their molecular structure. He was particularly interested in

▲ *Though Pasteur's wife, Marie, was not trained as a scientist, she was one of her husband's most important collaborators, insulating him from the distractions of day-to-day life and taking detailed notes for him.*

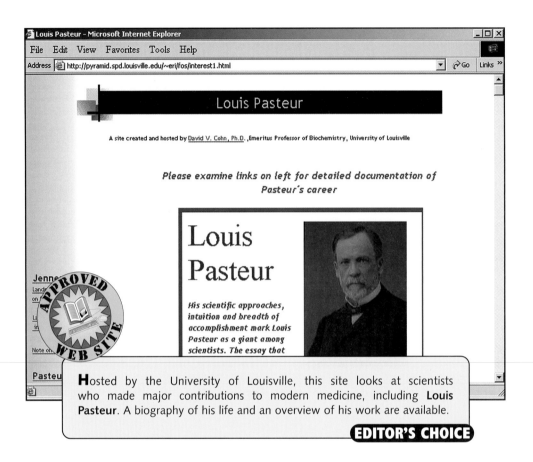

Louis Pasteur - Microsoft Internet Explorer

File   Edit   View   Favorites   Tools   Help

Address http://pyramid.spd.louisville.edu/~eri/fos/interest1.html

Louis Pasteur

A site created and hosted by David V. Cohn, Ph.D., Emeritus Professor of Biochemistry, University of Louisville

Please examine links on left for detailed documentation of Pasteur's career

Louis Pasteur

His scientific approaches, intuition and breadth of accomplishment mark Louis Pasteur as a giant among scientists. The essay that

Hosted by the University of Louisville, this site looks at scientists who made major contributions to modern medicine, including **Louis Pasteur**. A biography of his life and an overview of his work are available.

EDITOR'S CHOICE

quinine, quinidine, and cinchonia, drugs known to reduce fevers. These three drugs had been developed from the bark of the cinchona tree, which had been discovered in South America in 1820 but used by South American Indians tribes for centuries.

In 1851, the Society of Pharmacy of Paris promised a prize to any scientist who could create racemic acid out of tartaric acid. Pasteur was intrigued by the challenge. In the course of his experiments, he discovered that on the molecular level, quinidine was the right-handed version of quinine. He also learned that heating the substances changed their molecular structure.

One day, Pasteur combined cinchonia and tartaric acid and heated the mixture. To his surprise, the tartaric acid turned into racemic acid. Pasteur published the results of this experiment. In 1853, the Society of Pharmacy awarded Pasteur the 1,500-franc prize, money he used to buy new equipment for his laboratory.

→ MYSTERY OF FERMENTATION

In 1854, Pasteur was appointed professor of chemistry and dean of the Faculty of Sciences at the University of Lille in northern France. That fall, Pasteur moved his family to Lille, at the time, the fifth-largest city in France and a thriving center of industry. It was just the sort of place that appealed to Pasteur.

The director of education at the university was not especially sympathetic to the notion of science for the sake of science and Pasteur was only too happy to make his scientific expertise available to local industry. According to Pasteur, "There does not exist a category of science to which one can give the name applied science. There are science and the applications of science, bound together as the fruit of the tree which bears it."[4]

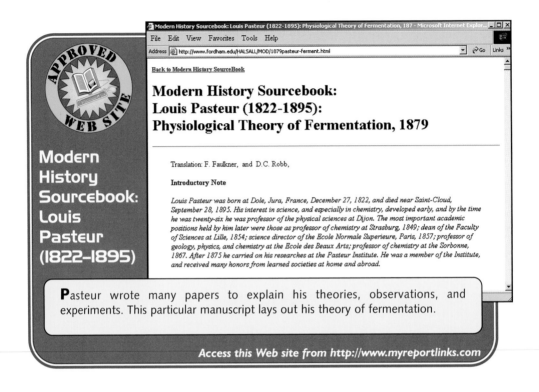

Modern History Sourcebook: Louis Pasteur (1822-1895): Physiological Theory of Fermentation, 187 – Microsoft Internet Explor...

File   Edit   View   Favorites   Tools   Help

Address http://www.fordham.edu/HALSALL/MOD/1879pasteur-ferment.html   Go   Links »

Back to Modern History SourceBook

Modern History Sourcebook:
Louis Pasteur (1822-1895):
Physiological Theory of Fermentation, 1879

Translation: F. Faulkner, and D.C. Robb,

Introductory Note

Louis Pasteur was born at Dole, Jura, France, December 27, 1822, and died near Saint-Cloud, September 28, 1895. His interest in science, and especially in chemistry, developed early, and by the time he was twenty-six he was professor of the physical sciences at Dijon. The most important academic positions held by him later were those as professor of chemistry at Strasburg, 1849; dean of the Faculty of Sciences at Lille, 1854; science director of the Ecole Normale Superieure, Paris, 1857; professor of geology, physics, and chemistry at the Ecole des Beaux Arts; professor of chemistry at the Sorbonne, 1867. After 1875 he carried on his researches at the Pasteur Institute. He was a member of the Institute, and received many honors from learned societies at home and abroad.

Modern History Sourcebook: Louis Pasteur (1822-1895)

Pasteur wrote many papers to explain his theories, observations, and experiments. This particular manuscript lays out his theory of fermentation.

Access this Web site from http://www.myreportlinks.com

In a speech delivered to a group of businessmen in Lille, Pasteur highlighted the practical advantages of a science education. He said, "Where . . . will you find a young man whose curiosity and interest will not immediately be awakened when you put into his hands a potato, and when with that potato he may produce sugar, and with that sugar alcohol, and that alcohol ether and vinegar?"[5]

Once Pasteur began teaching chemistry at Lille, hundreds of new students were attracted to the university. The courses emphasized the practical applications of science, so Pasteur took his students on tours of coal mines, distilleries, breweries, chemical plants, and textile mills. He wanted his students to see science at work in various manufacturing processes.

Soon enough, Pasteur had the opportunity to put his ideas to practical use. In 1856, a man named Bigot, the father of one of Pasteur's chemistry students, came to see Pasteur. Bigot was involved in the production of beet-root alcohol. Pure alcohol can be produced from beets through a chemical process known as fermentation and its production was one of the most important industries in the region. Bigot complained to Pasteur that he and others in his industry had some serious problems with the production of their beet-root alcohol. Often the alcohol was of poor quality and had an acidic or sour taste, and sometimes lactic acid would form. The vats in which the sugar-beet liquid turned into alcohol gave off terrible smells. Bigot hoped Pasteur could help.

⊛ Sour Grapes

Pasteur threw himself into the riddle of alcoholic fermentation. At the time, scientists believed that it was a purely chemical process. The breakdown of sugar into alcohol was thought to be due to the presence of certain unstabilizing "vibrations." But Pasteur had a hunch that, since yeast was somehow involved, fermentation might be biological and not chemical. Scientists

Pasteur was infamous for keeping very detailed notes of his observations and experiments. However, he was also secretive, and his notebooks weren't made public until almost eighty years after his death.

...ister _____, le virus rabique le plus virulent,

virus qui donne la rage aux lapins après 7 jours d'incubation,

...dont j'ai parlé autorisait cette entreprise.

...16 juillet, on peut sans inconvénient inoculer les virus les plus

...la consolidation de l'état réfractaire à la rage.

Joseph Meister. Elle n'a jamais rien laissé à désirer, à part

...et qui n'ont jamais empêché le sommeil et l'appétit.

~~de faire connaître~~ capable de prévenir la rage après morsure ?

de toutes sortes sur la rage je rencontrai bon nombre de circonstances

Voici les plus significatifs :

...dans les cas où les quantités inoculées sont considérables,

...dans un peu de liquide stérilisé, et en se servant des virus

...est rendu réfractaire à la maladie de par le fait de

...ibles. Au contraire, une inoculation particulière, qui n'introduit sous la peau même qu'une quantité de virus très faible

...qui se déclarent paraît diminuer quand les quantités de virus

à la suite des inoculations hypodermiques

quand elles ne le donnent pas, il n'y a pas d'état réfractaire.

...ème ordre me persuadèrent que ces faits paraîtraient moins étranges

...rabique est formé de deux matières, l'une pouvant

...et d'une matière non vivante qui aurait la

...le, par conséquent, dans des conditions déterminées, d'empêcher

en outre que la virulence rabique a une longue durée

...alogues perdent beaucoup de leur singularité.

...phylaxie dont je viens de parler semble démontrer,

...atière préservatrice en question.

...rvative _____ limite beaucoup la durée de

...clater à la suite du traitement par un défaut d'immunité, elle se déclarerait

...milieu du mois d'août, j'étais rassuré sur l'avenir de la santé de

...on accident du 4 juillet, ne prouverait plus contre le danger de sa morsure. Les très longues

...exemple fort authentique. La commission de la rage a fait mordre ce lundi neuf le 12 mai dernier qui a été

...par la désanation. Ces deux lapins sont morts simultanément pris de rage le 15ème jour après leur inoculation.

were aware that yeast, a tiny one-celled living organism, had *something* to do with fermentation, they did not know exactly *what*. Pasteur intended to find out.

Pasteur believed that the fermentation that causes milk to go sour occurs when lactose, the sugar in milk, is changed into lactic acid, a syrupy liquid. Once he began to experiment with lactic acid and observed the lactic yeast through his microscope, he became convinced.

➡ACID OR ALCOHOL?

When Pasteur studied the alcohol from Bigot's factory through the microscope, he saw that the yeast cells were plump and budding. But when lactic acid formed instead of alcohol, small rod-like microbes were always mixed with the yeast cells. Pasteur also observed other compounds being formed during fermentation. And some of these compounds rotated light, meaning they were asymmetric. Pasteur believed that only living cells produced asymmetric compounds. He concluded that living cells, the yeast, were responsible for forming alcohol from sugar. He also concluded that contaminating microorganisms were causing the fermented products to go sour at Bigot's factory.

In August 1857, Pasteur presented a paper on lactic acid fermentation. In it, he wrote that microbes—or microscopic organisms—cause fermentation, and specific kinds of microbes cause specific types of fermentation. The ideas in this paper came to be known as the germ theory of fermentation.

⊖ SPONTANEOUS GENERATION

In October 1857, Pasteur was appointed administrator and director of scientific studies at his old school, the École Normale Supérieure in Paris. Unfortunately, the school did not provide him with a laboratory. Since he had little funding for his work, he set up a lab in two tiny attic rooms at the school. In a cramped space, under less than ideal working conditions, Pasteur forged ahead with his research and experiments. For the next twenty years, he would continue to learn more about fermentation. But he would also devote time and energy to other scientific challenges.

In 1859, tragedy struck. Pasteur's oldest daughter, Jeanne, died of typhoid fever. She had been visiting her grandfather at Arbois when she became ill. Pasteur was devastated and sought comfort in his work. To Marie, who was still in Arbois, he wrote, "Yes, when you come back, I wish that between us, with us, there will be nothing but our love, our children, their upbringing, their future, along with my dreams of science. For you, for them, life will be made beautiful by my work, by the success of new discoveries, and by generous feelings."[6]

In 1860, the French Academy of Sciences offered a cash prize to any scientist who could shed new light on the question of spontaneous generation. There had been a furious debate raging between those who believed in spontaneous generation and those who did not. The academy wanted the matter settled.

Pasteur accepted the challenge, understanding that the issue was somehow related to his experiments with fermentation. He wrote that, "Among the questions raised by my research on the ferments in the narrow sense, none are more worthy of attention than those relating to the origin of

APPROVED WEB SITE

A Traveler's Guide to the History of Biology and Medicine

A Traveler's Guide to the History of Biology and Medicine - Microsoft Internet Explorer

File   Edit   View   Favorites   Tools   Help

Address   http://www.historyofbiologyandmedicine.com/index.html   Go   Links »

"A Traveler's Guide to the History of Biology and Medicine"
(1986) by Dr. Eric T. (Ted) Pengelley

HOME   INTRODUCTION

Britain France West Germany Italy Switzerland Austria Czechoslovakia Hungary Holland Sweden United States Canada

Prior to embarking for Europe for a medical conference in 1999, I was handed a book by one of my surgical residents entitled, "A Traveler's Guide to the History of Biology and Medicine" (1986) by Dr. Eric T. (Ted) Pengelley. As I had already planned on touring some historical sites during my trip, I packed the guide and on the flight read the section on Italy, my intended destination. Intrigued by what I read, I visited three of the featured sites in the guide and found their descriptions to be highly accurate and informative. I felt that I had gained much from incorporating these sites into my trip and that the guide's information greatly enhanced the experience of the actual visit.

Eager to learn more, I finished Pengelley's guide upon my return to the United States. However, on subsequent trips both here and abroad, I found that some of the information in the guide was dated or changed. I researched to see if another edition of the guide was available, and my search led me directly to the author himself. I contacted Dr. Pengelley directly and was quite pleased when he graciously accepted my call.

During our conversation, he informed me he was no longer interested in updating the guide because his wife Daphne, who had co-authored the book, had passed away some years

rewrite

This Web site offers a guide to travelers interested in visiting sites in Europe and North America that have a place in the history of medicine.

Access this Web site from http://www.myreportlinks.com

the ferments. Where do they come from, these mysterious agents, so feeble in appearance yet so powerful in reality . . . this is the problem that has led me to study the so-called spontaneous generations."[7]

⇒ OUT OF THIN AIR

For thousands of years, from ancient times through the Middle Ages and the Renaissance, people believed that certain living organisms could be spontaneously generated. They thought such organisms could be created by the soil or the sun—or even arise out of the air. In the 1600s, a Flemish scholar named Jan Baptista van Helmont claimed that frogs sprang from the miasma of marshes. He also described the result of another experiment he claimed proved spontaneous generation: "If one presses a dirty shirt into the opening of a vessel containing grains of wheat, the ferment from the dirty shirt does not modify the smell of the grain but gives rise to the transmutation of the wheat into mice after about twenty-one days."[8]

In the eighteenth century, an Englishman named John Needham theorized that a "life force" present in all nonliving things caused new organisms to spring to life. To prove his theory, Needham boiled chicken soup and poured it into a glass flask, sealing the flask with a cork. A few

Pasteur worked constantly during his life, even while on vacation. Shown here, his lab at his home in Arbois, where he spent time in the summer.

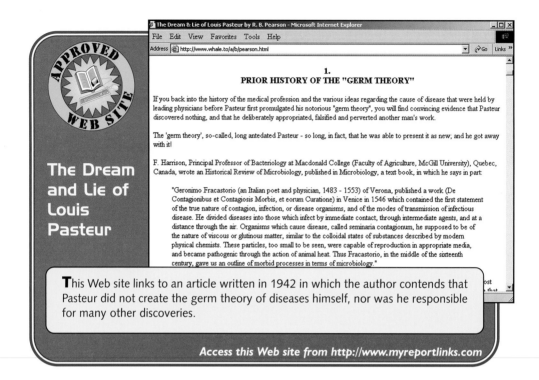

The Dream and Lie of Louis Pasteur

The Dream & Lie of Louis Pasteur by R. B. Pearson - Microsoft Internet Explorer

File   Edit   View   Favorites   Tools   Help

Address 🗟 http://www.whale.to/a/b/pearson.html

1.

PRIOR HISTORY OF THE "GERM THEORY"

If you back into the history of the medical profession and the various ideas regarding the cause of disease that were held by leading physicians before Pasteur first promulgated his notorious "germ theory", you will find convincing evidence that Pasteur discovered nothing, and that he deliberately appropriated, falsified and perverted another man's work.

The 'germ theory', so-called, long antedated Pasteur - so long, in fact, that he was able to present it as new; and he got away with it!

F. Harrison, Principal Professor of Bacteriology at Macdonald College (Faculty of Agriculture, McGill University), Quebec, Canada, wrote an Historical Review of Microbiology, published in Microbiology, a text book, in which he says in part:

"Geronimo Fracastorio (an Italian poet and physician, 1483 - 1553) of Verona, published a work (De Contagionibus et Contagiosis Morbis, et eorum Curatione) in Venice in 1546 which contained the first statement of the true nature of contagion, infection, or disease organisms, and of the modes of transmission of infectious disease. He divided diseases into those which infect by immediate contact, through intermediate agents, and at a distance through the air. Organisms which cause disease, called seminaria contagionum, he supposed to be of the nature of viscous or glutinous matter, similar to the colloidal states of substances described by modern physical chemists. These particles, too small to be seen, were capable of reproduction in appropriate media, and became pathogenic through the action of animal heat. Thus Fracastorio, in the middle of the sixteenth century, gave us an outline of morbid processes in terms of microbiology."

This Web site links to an article written in 1942 in which the author contends that Pasteur did not create the germ theory of diseases himself, nor was he responsible for many other discoveries.

Access this Web site from http://www.myreportlinks.com

days later he saw that the broth was full of microorganisms. Needham then claimed he had proved the existence of spontaneous generation. Lazzaro Spallanzani, an Italian physiologist, repeated the experiment and got the same results. However, when he carried out the experiment again, sealing the flask shut more tightly, nothing grew.

By the 1800s, most scientists no longer believed that frogs, mice, or any other visible creature could spring to life as a result of spontaneous generation. But they still believed that microscopic organisms did. As late as 1859, a scientist named Félix-Archimède Pouchet published a book that claimed spontaneous generation was real. Pasteur suspected these scientists were wrong.

Based on his work on fermentation, Pasteur thought it was obvious that the yeast and other microbes entered from outside, carried by dust particles in the air. Still, he had to prove it. So he did.

⊛ THE MYTH OF SPONTANEOUS GENERATION

Pasteur filled several flasks, or bottles, with boiled liquid and sealed them. He then took them to various locations and briefly unsealed them, exposing the liquid inside to the air. When he observed them again back in his laboratory, microorganisms were growing inside. A short time later, Pasteur noted that the flasks that had been opened in dusty areas contained more microbes, demonstrating that the microbes had been carried by particles of dust in the air.

Pasteur repeated his experiment, but this time he used swan-necked flasks, the necks bent in such a way that they resembled the neck of a swan. Again, he boiled the liquid inside the flasks, but this time, he did not seal them. As he expected, the liquid remained free of microbes. Air had entered the flasks but the microorganisms in the air had become trapped in the bend of the neck. Pasteur then tilted the flasks, allowing the liquid inside to pour into the bend of the neck.

This caused the liquid to become contaminated, and once again, microbes soon appeared. Pasteur's experiment had proved that the microbes had not been spontaneously generated.

On April 7, 1864, Pasteur described his experiments in a speech at the Sorbonne University in Paris. He concluded by saying:

A bust of Pasteur surrounded by items symbolic of his career, including a bottle of wine, a microscope and a few pages from the many notebooks he filled.

. . . Gentlemen, I could point to that liquid and say to you, I have taken my drop of water from the immensity of creation, and I have taken it full of the elements appropriated to the development of inferior beings. And I wait, I watch, I question it, begging it to recommence for me the beautiful spectacle of the first creation. But it is dumb, dumb since these experiments were begun several years ago; it is dumb because I have kept it from the only thing man does not know how to produce, from the germs which float in the air, from Life, for Life is a germ and a germ is Life. Never will the doctrine of spontaneous generation recover from the mortal blow of this simple experiment.[9]

Pasteur had been elected to the Academy of Sciences in 1862 for his discoveries. In 1864, the academy awarded him its 2,500-franc prize for proving that spontaneous generation did not exist.

➔ RESCUING THE WINE INDUSTRY

In 1863, Louis-Napoléon (also known as Emperor Napoléon III), the ruler of France, became aware of serious problems in the wine industry, crucial to the French economy. Winemakers reported that, for unknown reasons, their wine was often spoiled. Merchants were canceling orders, complaining that the wine was often sour or bitter. Louis-Napoléon could not allow one of France's most important industries to fail. One of his advisors suggested that he ask Pasteur, already famous

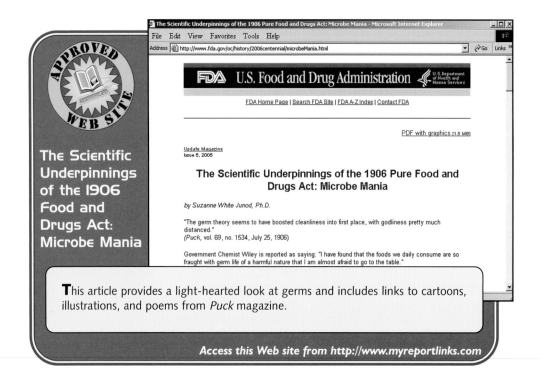

The Scientific Underpinnings of the 1906 Food and Drugs Act: Microbe Mania

The Scientific Underpinnings of the 1906 Pure Food and Drugs Act: Microbe Mania - Microsoft Internet Explorer

File   Edit   View   Favorites   Tools   Help

Address http://www.fda.gov/oc/history/2006centennial/microbeMania.html   Go Links »

FDA U.S. Food and Drug Administration U.S. Department of Health and Human Services

FDA Home Page | Search FDA Site | FDA A-Z Index | Contact FDA

PDF with graphics (1.5 MB)

Update Magazine
Issue 5, 2005

The Scientific Underpinnings of the 1906 Pure Food and Drugs Act: Microbe Mania

by Suzanne White Junod, Ph.D.

"The germ theory seems to have boosted cleanliness into first place, with godliness pretty much distanced."
(Puck, vol. 69, no. 1534, July 25, 1906)

Government Chemist Wiley is reported as saying: "I have found that the foods we daily consume are so fraught with germ life of a harmful nature that I am almost afraid to go to the table."

This article provides a light-hearted look at germs and includes links to cartoons, illustrations, and poems from *Puck* magazine.

Access this Web site from http://www.myreportlinks.com

for his work on fermentation, to help. Pasteur quickly agreed.

Pasteur spent the summers of 1863, 1864, and 1865 in the vineyards around Arbois. Thinking back to what he had learned from his work with beet-juice alcohol, Pasteur suspected that microorganisms were causing the wine to spoil. He knew that certain bacteria in the fermentation process turned alcohol into vinegar. Perhaps the same bacteria were causing the wine to go sour. Pasteur studied many samples of wine and discovered that the bacteria known as *Mycoderma aceti* was responsible for most of the problems.

Pasteur remembered that heating had killed bacteria during fermentation. So he heated the wine for a few minutes without air. Too little heat would not be effective; too much heat would ruin the wine. After experimenting, Pasteur found that heating the wine after fermentation to 55°C (131°F, or just below the boiling point), would get rid of the harmful bacteria and not affect the taste.

Pasteur's process of the sterilization of liquids after fermentation was named for him: pasteurization. Winemakers throughout France, and then in other countries, began using the process. Producers of beer, vinegar, milk, cheese and other foods that easily spoiled would later use pasteurization.

ANGEROUS MICROORGANISMS

On June 15, 1865, Pasteur's father, Jean-Joseph, died. He was seventy-four years old. Three months later, on September 11, Camille, the scientist's youngest daughter, died. She was only two. Then, just a few months later, on May 23, 1866, his daughter Cécile died of typhoid fever. Pasteur was heartbroken.

But even more, Pasteur was bitter that medical science had not advanced enough to save the people he loved. Pasteur already suspected that microorganisms were involved in infection and disease. More than anything else, he was desperate to find ways to lessen the human suffering caused by these tiny germs, he wanted to protect people from dangerous microorganisms. But before he could do that, there was another French industry that needed his help.

SAVING THE SILKWORMS

CHAPTER

6

In 1865, Pasteur's friend and former professor, Jean-Baptiste Dumas, had written to Pasteur, telling him that some sort of epidemic was killing the silkworms in southern France. If something was not done, the silk industry, like wine an important part of France's economy, could disappear.

Dumas, now a member of the French government, pleaded with Pasteur to help. Dumas was joined in his appeal by Emperor Louis-Napoléon. Pasteur could not refuse and he quickly learned all he could about the life cycle of silkworms. In June 1865, he traveled to Alès in the heart of the silkworm region in the south of France, where he met with silkworm breeders. Pasteur set up a field laboratory and spent the next four summers there conducting research.

Silkworms and the mulberry trees on which they feed had been brought to southern France from China during the Middle Ages. By the 1800s, the country produced about ten percent of the world's silk. The silkworm, the larva or caterpillar stage of a moth, hatches from eggs

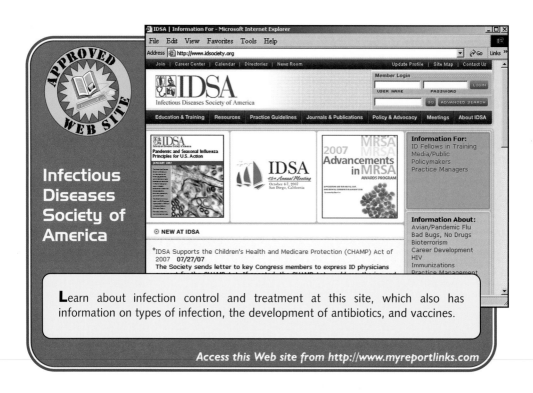

Infectious
Diseases
Society of
America

Learn about infection control and treatment at this site, which also has information on types of infection, the development of antibiotics, and vaccines.

Access this Web site from http://www.myreportlinks.com

that the silk moth lays. As the silkworm grows, it spins a cocoon around itself—silk is made from the thread of the cocoon. The silkworm eventually emerges from the cocoon as an adult moth.

A few days after his arrival in Alès, Pasteur got word that his father was gravely ill. Pasteur left immediately, but his father had died by the time he reached Arbois. Pasteur returned to Alès, determined to carry out his important research.

Pasteur examined both healthy and unhealthy silkworms that had small black spots on their skin. The sick worms had a disease called pébrine, French slang for "pepper," because the spots resembled grains of pepper. In the sick silkworms, Pasteur saw oval shapes through his microscope. He suspected that these were some type of microorganism that was passed from the parent moths to the caterpillar young.

Pasteur advised the silkworm breeders to cut open adult moths after the eggs were laid and examine tissue samples under a microscope. If the adults moths had the dangerous microbes, their eggs were diseased and should be destroyed. If there were no microbes, then the eggs were healthy.

The breeders complained that they would never be able to learn to use an instrument as complicated as a microscope. Pasteur told them, "There is in my laboratory a little girl eight years of age who has learned to use it without difficulty."[1] The little girl Pasteur was referring to was his daughter Marie-Louise, who had been examining moths along with her mother.

⊘Looks Can Be Deceiving

The breeders followed Pasteur's instructions, but they discovered another problem: Sick caterpillars had hatched from eggs that seemed to be healthy. Pasteur then realized that the microbes he had observed were not germs, but parasites, or organisms that live in and feed on other organisms. In addition to being passed from parents to eggs, the

Pasteur, (front row, third-from-left), receives most of the credit for his many discoveries, but the reality is that he had a lot of help. Here he is seated with some of his collaborators.

parasites were contagious, meaning they could spread disease from a sick caterpillar to a healthy one.

⊘ Life Goes On

During the next two summers and despite great personal tragedy, Pasteur worked long and hard trying to solve the silkworm problem. He oversaw the entire process, from raising silkworms, to collecting their eggs, to harvesting mulberry leaves. He ran experiment after experiment. Finally, he discovered that the silkworms were being affected by another contagious disease called flacherie.

Pasteur now knew that France's silkworms were threatened by a deadly combination of two contagious diseases. When he studied mulberry leaves through his microscope, he observed the flacherie germs growing in the folds and creases of the leaves. A healthy caterpillar eating the contaminated leaves would therefore get sick.

Pasteur instructed the silkworm breeders to separate infected caterpillars from healthy ones and make sure to keep the caterpillars' food, the mulberry leaves, clean. The breeders followed Pasteur's simple advice, and the silkworms were saved. Before long, the silk industry in France, so important to its economy, was recovering.

At the same time he was focused on the silkworm, Pasteur had been working during the fall and winter back in Paris. In 1867, his position with the École Normale changed, and he was named director of a new chemistry laboratory, which he had requested and which had been built especially for him when he accepted his job at the Sorbonne.

⊜ SPREAD THIN

Holding two jobs in Paris while he worked hard in southern France may have taken a toll on Pasteur's health—on October 19, 1868, he suffered a stroke. It paralyzed the left side of his body. Pasteur slowly recovered from the paralysis, but for the rest of his life, his speech and ability to walk were never the same. Maybe even more devastating to

Le Petit Journal

Le Petit Journal
CHAQUE JOUR 5 CENTIMES

Le Supplément illustré
CHAQUE SEMAINE 5 CENTIMES

SUPPLÉMENT ILLUSTRÉ
Huit pages : CINQ centimes

ABONNEMENTS
—
	TROIS MOIS	SIX MOIS	UN AN
SEINE ET SEINE-ET-OISE	1 fr.	2 fr.	3 fr. 50
DÉPARTEMENTS	1 fr.	2 fr.	4 fr.
ÉTRANGER	1 50	2 50	5 fr.

Sixième année — DIMANCHE 13 OCTOBRE 1895 — Numéro 256

A LOUIS PASTEUR

△ *Though honored when he died in 1895, as he was here by this French publication, Pasteur was equally celebrated during his lifetime.*

the scientist, Pasteur never regained full use of his hands, which meant that he had to rely on assistants in the lab.

In November 1869, Emperor Louis-Napoléon and his wife, the Empress Eugenie, invited Pasteur and his family to stay at Villa Vicentina, their estate in Trieste. While resting there, Pasteur noticed the many mulberry trees on the estate. The area had been known for its silk production until the pébrine and flacherie diseases had ruined it. Pasteur reestablished silk breeding on the estate. He also wrote *Studies on the Disease of the Silkworm,* which he dedicated to the Empress Eugenie. The book, which was published in 1870, was used for years by

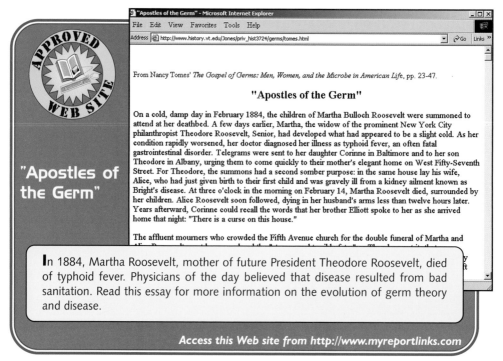

"Apostles of the Germ"

APPROVED WEB SITE

"Apostles of the Germ" - Microsoft Internet Explorer

File   Edit   View   Favorites   Tools   Help

Address http://www.history.vt.edu/Jones/priv_hist3724/germs/tomes.html

From Nancy Tomes' *The Gospel of Germs: Men, Women, and the Microbe in American Life,* pp. 23-47.

"Apostles of the Germ"

On a cold, damp day in February 1884, the children of Martha Bulloch Roosevelt were summoned to attend at her deathbed. A few days earlier, Martha, the widow of the prominent New York City philanthropist Theodore Roosevelt, Senior, had developed what had appeared to be a slight cold. As her condition rapidly worsened, her doctor diagnosed her illness as typhoid fever, an often fatal gastrointestinal disorder. Telegrams were sent to her daughter Corinne in Baltimore and to her son Theodore in Albany, urging them to come quickly to their mother's elegant home on West Fifty-Seventh Street. For Theodore, the summons had a second somber purpose: in the same house lay his wife, Alice, who had just given birth to their first child and was gravely ill from a kidney ailment known as Bright's disease. At three o'clock in the morning on February 14, Martha Roosevelt died, surrounded by her children. Alice Roosevelt soon followed, dying in her husband's arms less than twelve hours later. Years afterward, Corinne could recall the words that her brother Elliott spoke to her as she arrived home that night: "There is a curse on this house."

The affluent mourners who crowded the Fifth Avenue church for the double funeral of Martha and

In 1884, Martha Roosevelt, mother of future President Theodore Roosevelt, died of typhoid fever. Physicians of the day believed that disease resulted from bad sanitation. Read this essay for more information on the evolution of germ theory and disease.

Access this Web site from http://www.myreportlinks.com

other scientists studying infectious diseases in animals.

⊜ FRANCE GOES TO WAR

In the early summer of 1870, Pasteur returned to Paris from Trieste, eager to begin research and experiments to learn more about the nature of infectious diseases. But on July 15, 1870, France declared war on Prussia, a part of the German Empire. The war delayed Pasteur's plans indefinitely.

Because of the example set by his father, Pasteur had grown up with a deep love for France and strong feelings about the honor and glory of Emperor Napoléon I. As a patriot, Pasteur would certainly have volunteered to join the army and fight for his country. But his physical condition after his stroke prevented him from doing that. However, the scientist's patriotism had been conveyed to his children and his son, Jean-Baptiste, joined the army.

Very early in the fighting, it was clear that France had suffered a humiliating defeat. Paris was under siege and food supplies were cut off. Pasteur, his wife and their daughter fled Paris, barely getting out before the city was struck by a terrible famine. The family retreated to Arbois, thinking they would be safe there. But before long, Germans occupied the town. The Pasteurs fled again, this time to southern France.

Four months later, Paris surrendered and the siege ended. But the war was not over and by January 1871, the Pasteurs, who had not received any news from Jean-Baptiste in quite some time, set off in search of him. They traveled through the snowy forests in the area where Jean-Baptiste's regiment had last been seen. Finally, they came across a soldier who told them where they could find Jean-Baptiste.

the time line: Science, "society", and immunity - Microsoft Internet Explorer

File Edit View Favorites Tools Help

Address http://pubs.acs.org/subscribe/journals/mdd/v04/i10/html/10timeline.html

thetimeline

CHRISTOPHER S. W. KOEHLER

Science, "society", and immunity

The evolution of vaccines and antitoxins was a collaboration between hard science and the social milieu.

mdd
Proteomics

October 2001
Vol. 4, No. 10, pp 59–60.

Table of Contents

MDD Home

Contact Us

The earliest known attempts to produce artificial immunity to disease involved smallpox, one of the great diseases of history. It disfigured or killed people of all social classes, from kings to commoners; and many cultures tried to stop it by inducing immunity. In China, powdered smallpox scabs were blown into the sinuses, and a century before Edward Jenner, Chinese physicians prepared pills made from the fleas of cows in an effort to prevent the disease. In India, physicians conferred immunity by applying scabs to the scarified skin of the healthy. The technique spread west along the silk road to Istanbul, where it came to Western attention.

A doctor in 19th-century England vaccinates children against smallpox. CORBIS

Speckled monster

New vaccines are often controversial, even feared. The author of this essay, **The Timeline: Science, "Society", and Immunity**, addresses how treatments come to be accepted in part as a result of the collaboration of science and society.

Jean-Baptiste, suffering from malnutrition and exhaustion, was too weak to walk. He was being carried on a cart. The Pasteurs nursed him back to health and he was able to rejoin his regiment until the war ended.

The Franco-Prussian War ended when France signed the Treaty of Frankfurt in May 1871. Emperor Louis-Napoléon surrendered to William I of Prussia. The French people demanded that the emperor step down and allow the election of new leaders. Pasteur was enraged.

⊜ Better Brew

In 1868, the University of Bonn in Germany had given Pasteur an honorary degree. After France's surrender, he returned the diploma, saying the sight of it made him sick. He was also angry at French officials, blaming them for not giving enough support to the sciences: Pasteur believed that France would have been much stronger and better able to defend itself if it had spent more money and paid more attention to advancements in science.

Pasteur expressed his frustration in the best way he knew how—through science. Germany was known for its excellent beer and the scientist was determined to help French breweries produce a product that was at least equal to German beer. As he had done with the French wine industry,

Pasteur was able to prove that microorganisms were compromising French beer. He showed the brewers how they could solve the problem, inventing a process for pasteurizing beer.

⊖ GERM THEORY

By 1871, Pasteur had completed his work on silkworms and had solved the problems of wine-making and beer production. He enjoyed those challenges but he was now ready to turn his thoughts to another set of problems that had long bothered him: the causes and prevention of human diseases. He knew, however, that he would need a lot of time in order to properly study these huge questions. With that in mind, he resigned from the École Normale Supérieure, citing concerns about his health (though he remained as director of his laboratory there).

Pasteur's accomplishments had already made him a famous chemist. But he needed credibility in the medical world before doctors and surgeons would take his ideas seriously, so he campaigned for election to the Academy of Medicine, whose membership consisted of doctors and pharmacists. On March 25, 1873, Pasteur was admitted as an associate member of the Academy of Medicine.

All of Pasteur's work up to this time had convinced him that microorganisms, or germs, were the cause of disease. He also believed that germs were transmitted more easily under unsanitary conditions and through carelessness and ignorance. Pasteur set out to test his belief by visiting hospitals. He was amazed—the conditions were terrible, with most hospitals overcrowded and infested with germs that caused infections that often led to death.

⇒ BAD MEDICINE

Pasteur spoke with doctors and the people who ran hospitals to learn more. Initially, he assumed that patients were most threatened by microorganisms in the air, but he changed his mind. He came to believe that patients were, in fact, being made even sicker by the people taking care of them—doctors, nurses, and others. He presented his thesis in a famous lecture he delivered at the Academy of Medicine.

> This water, this sponge, this lint with which you wash or cover a wound, deposit germs which have the power of multiplying rapidly within the tissues and which would invariably cause the death of the patient in a very short time, if the vital processes of the body did not counteract them. But alas, the vital resistance is too often impotent. . . . If I had the honor of being a surgeon, impressed as I am with the dangers to which the patient is exposed by the microbes present over the surface of all objects, particularly in hospitals, not only would I use none but perfectly clean instruments. . . .

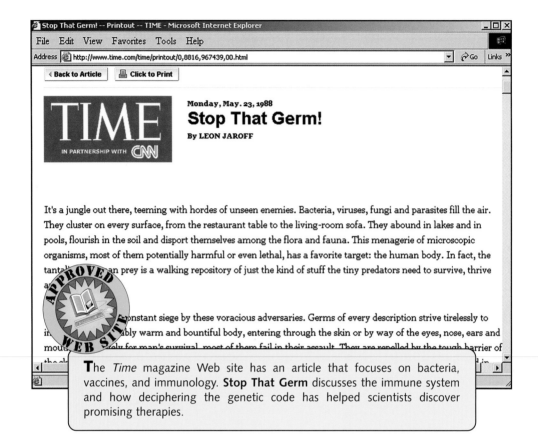

Stop That Germ! -- Printout -- TIME - Microsoft Internet Explorer

File Edit View Favorites Tools Help

Address http://www.time.com/time/printout/0,8816,967439,00.html Go Links »

‹ Back to Article   Click to Print

TIME
IN PARTNERSHIP WITH CNN

Monday, May. 23, 1988
Stop That Germ!
By LEON JAROFF

It's a jungle out there, teeming with hordes of unseen enemies. Bacteria, viruses, fungi and parasites fill the air. They cluster on every surface, from the restaurant table to the living-room sofa. They abound in lakes and in pools, flourish in the soil and disport themselves among the flora and fauna. This menagerie of microscopic organisms, most of them potentially harmful or even lethal, has a favorite target: the human body. In fact, the tant... an prey is a walking repository of just the kind of stuff the tiny predators need to survive, thrive

...nstant siege by these voracious adversaries. Germs of every description strive tirelessly to ...bly warm and bountiful body, entering through the skin or by way of the eyes, nose, ears and mout... ...ly for man's survival, most of them fail in their assault. They are repelled by the tough barrier of the ...

The *Time* magazine Web site has an article that focuses on bacteria, vaccines, and immunology. **Stop That Germ** discusses the immune system and how deciphering the genetic code has helped scientists discover promising therapies.

I would use only lint, bandages and sponges previously exposed to a temperature of 130 degrees to 150 degrees C.[2]

→ DOUBTING DOCTORS

At first, most doctors dismissed Pasteur's germ theory of disease as nonsense. After all, what did a chemist who had not gone to medical school know? But Pasteur persisted, making countless visits to hospitals, observing conditions in sickrooms, maternity wards, and operating rooms.

He examined blood samples. He then developed the first bacterial cultures from the blood samples. He hoped to determine the type of microbe that had caused a particular kind of infection. He tried to persuade doctors that the prevention of disease was just as important, if not more so, than treating disease.

Joseph Lister, a British surgeon working at the Glasgow Royal Infirmary in Scotland, was one of the few doctors who agreed with Pasteur's theory. He had followed the scientist's work for many years and had been impressed with his accomplishments. Lister began to sterilize his surgical instruments and bandages in carbolic acid. He and his assistants would also wash their hands in carbolic acid before operating. While operating, they sprayed an antiseptic mist of carbolic acid over the wound. The results were incredibly dramatic: The death rate of patients during surgery dropped from about 50 percent to less than three percent!

An Uphill Battle

In February 1874, Lister wrote to Pasteur and thanked him. Soon, other surgeons began to adopt cleaner habits. Unfortunately, most doctors refused to accept Pasteur's theory about the danger of contamination by microbes. They insisted that all the precautionary washing and cleaning was useless because germs did not cause diseases.

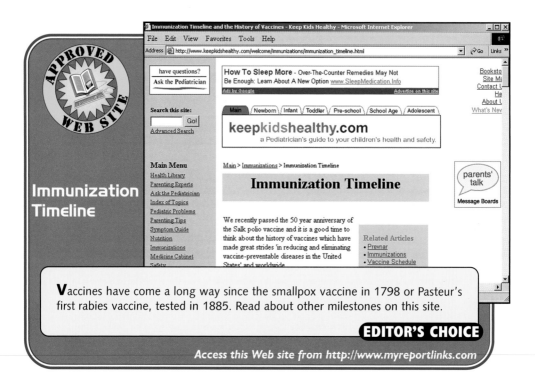

Immunization Timeline

Vaccines have come a long way since the smallpox vaccine in 1798 or Pasteur's first rabies vaccine, tested in 1885. Read about other milestones on this site.

EDITOR'S CHOICE

Access this Web site from http://www.myreportlinks.com

Pasteur remained steadfast in his beliefs and in 1878, he published his ideas about dangerous microbes in *The Theory of Germs and Its Applications to Medicine and Surgery.*

In May 1879, Pasteur attended a lecture by a doctor named Hervieux at the Academy of Medicine. Hervieux, speaking about an epidemic in maternity wards, claimed that microorganisms could not possibly be the cause, miasmas were.

Pasteur had heard enough. He interrupted Hervieux, saying, "What causes the epidemic is none of those things, it is the physician and his helpers who transport the microbe from a sick woman to a healthy woman."[3] Pasteur jumped out of his seat and up to the blackboard, where he drew a picture of a microbe in the form of chains. Pasteur had drawn a picture of what we now know is the streptococcus bacterium.

Over time, it became common accepted medical practice to sterilize dressings and instruments and wear sterile gloves and gowns during almost any medical procedure. But despite Pasteur's efforts, it would be several decades before such practice became routine.

⇒ FIGHTING THE MIGHTY GERM

By 1877, the focus of Pasteur's work was on the germ. He wanted to learn how and why germs actually caused disease. He hoped to discover a method to help people avoid infectious diseases altogether. But, before he could embark on this challenge, his country presented him with yet another.

In early 1877, the French minister of agriculture came to Pasteur with a pressing problem: hundreds of thousands of sheep in France and other European countries were being killed by anthrax, a disease that affects warm-blooded animals. Could Pasteur, who had saved the silkworm, stop the spread of anthrax?

Pasteur's ultimate goal was to find a way to prevent the spread of infectious disease in humans. But he understood that if he could learn

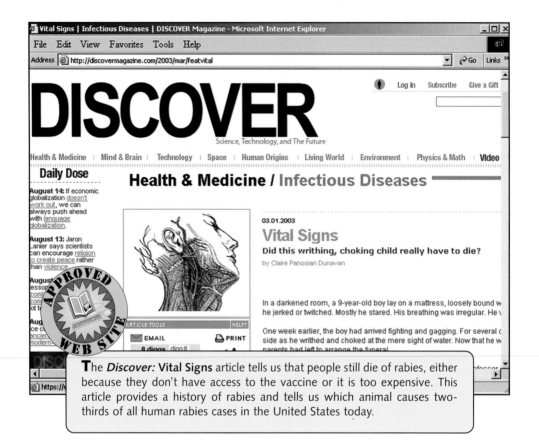

Vital Signs | Infectious Diseases | DISCOVER Magazine - Microsoft Internet Explorer

File   Edit   View   Favorites   Tools   Help

Address   http://discovermagazine.com/2003/mar/featvital   Go   Links

DISCOVER
Science, Technology, and The Future

Log In   Subscribe   Give a Gift

Health & Medicine | Mind & Brain | Technology | Space | Human Origins | Living World | Environment | Physics & Math | **Video**

Daily Dose

August 14: If economic globalization doesn't work out, we can always push ahead with language globalization.

August 13: Jaron Lanier says scientists can encourage religion to create peace rather than violence.

Health & Medicine / Infectious Diseases

03.01.2003

Vital Signs
Did this writhing, choking child really have to die?
by Claire Panosian Dunavan

In a darkened room, a 9-year-old boy lay on a mattress, loosely bound w he jerked or twitched. Mostly he stared. His breathing was irregular. He v

One week earlier, the boy had arrived fighting and gagging. For several c side as he writhed and choked at the mere sight of water. Now that he w parents had left to arrange the funeral.

ARTICLE TOOLS   HELP?

EMAIL   PRINT

digg digg it

The *Discover:* **Vital Signs** article tells us that people still die of rabies, either because they don't have access to the vaccine or it is too expensive. This article provides a history of rabies and tells us which animal causes two-thirds of all human rabies cases in the United States today.

how animals were affected by microbes, that knowledge would be useful in his battle against the microbes that attack humans. So once again, the patriotic Pasteur came to the aid of his country.

Robert Koch, a German scientist, had observed rod-shaped bacteria in the blood of animals afflicted with anthrax. He believed that anthrax was caused by this bacteria. In 1876, he published a paper describing his work. Most scientists did not accept Koch's ideas. But Pasteur believed he was on the right track and he intended to prove that the rod-shaped bacteria caused anthrax. First, he would need to learn how the disease was spread.

⟹ GOING AFTER ANTHRAX

Anthrax was (and still is) extremely deadly, a disease that can kill healthy victims in hours. Sometimes, humans who came in contact with infected animals also caught the disease. Pasteur took blood from a diseased sheep and thinned it. He then poured the mixture into a flask filled with a special liquid and repeated the process one hundred times. Finally, he injected the diluted blood into healthy rabbits and guinea pigs. The animals quickly developed anthrax and died. Clearly, the bacteria had survived despite being diluted one hundred times. With these experiments, Pasteur proved that the rod-shaped bacteria had caused anthrax.

⟹ COUNTING SHEEP

Next, Pasteur needed to learn how the livestock had become infected. He visited farms where sheep had been stricken. A farmer showed him spots in his field where he had buried sheep that had died of anthrax. Pasteur examined the soil at those spots. He noticed the mounds and tunnels built by earthworms. It occurred to him that the earthworms that fed on the buried sheep

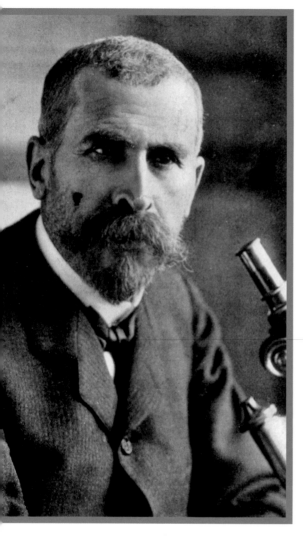

Emile Roux, who worked closely with Pasteur for many years, helped the scientist develop the first vaccines for anthrax, cholera, and rabies.

carried the anthrax bacteria from the dead sheep to the surface, poisoning the area where healthy sheep fed. Pasteur studied the worms and discovered that although they were not affected by the anthrax, the worms carried the virus and contaminated the soil.

Pasteur advised farmers to prevent their animals from grazing in fields where the dis-eased animals had been buried. He also urged them to burn the dead sheep instead of burying them. The farmers followed Pasteur's suggestions, which helped control the spread of anthrax; the death rate dropped dramatically. Still, Pasteur wanted to find a way to prevent an animal from getting anthrax, even if it were exposed to the disease.

⇒ CREATING IMMUNITY

In the spring of 1879, chicken cholera, another deadly disease, was spreading through the French countryside. Huge numbers of chickens were dying, and many farmers faced economic ruin. Pasteur began experimenting in his laboratory. He grew the bacteria in a mixture that he made from chicken meat and then injected healthy chickens with the chicken cholera bacteria. They soon died.

During the summer, Pasteur went on vacation. He left his assistant, Émile Roux, in charge of the chicken cholera cultures. When Pasteur returned, he continued his experiments, injecting bacteria into a few chickens that had been infected—and survived—before he had left on vacation. He also injected a few perfectly healthy chickens with bacteria. Not surprisingly, the chickens injected with just the fresh bacteria became sick and died. However, to Pasteur's amazement, those chickens that had previously received the dried-out cholera and then the fresh cholera remained healthy.

Pasteur concluded that the chickens survived because they had been vaccinated. He realized that the weakened bacteria had made the chickens immune to cholera. Pasteur theorized that animals, or people, that survived infection did so because they had built up an immunity to the microbe.

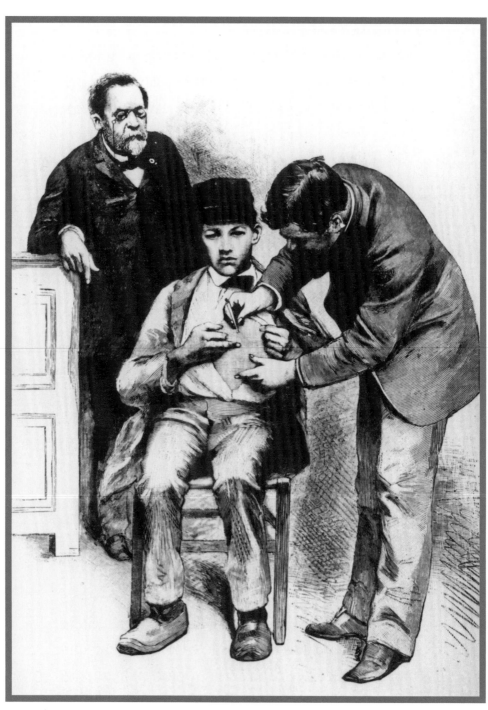

▲ *A drawing that appeared in a French magazine shows Pasteur watching as an assistant administers a shot of the rabies vaccine.*

⇒ CONQUERING CHOLERA

Pasteur was aware of the work of Edward Jenner, an English doctor who had given the first medical vaccination in 1796. Jenner had inoculated eight-year-old James Phipps with material that came from cowpox sores on the hand of a young girl. This girl had gotten cowpox, a virus, while milking a cow. Jenner inoculated Phipps again, this time with smallpox matter. Phipps and some others that Jenner inoculated never came down with smallpox. A friend of Jenner's named the process "vaccination," from the Latin word for cow, *vacca*.

In 1880, after some more experiments in his laboratory, Pasteur announced that he had created a vaccine for chicken cholera. "This is our chance," he said. "This is my most remarkable discovery— this is a *vaccine* that I've discovered. . . . We'll apply this to all . . . virulent diseases. . . . We will save lives!"[4]

⇒ ATTACKING ANTHRAX

Pasteur's next goal was to create vaccines for other diseases. By 1881, he had produced a vaccine for anthrax. On May 5, he held a demonstration at a farm at Pouilly le Fort. Pasteur inoculated twenty-four sheep, six cows, and one goat with a vaccine derived from a living weakened culture of anthrax bacillus, or bacteria.

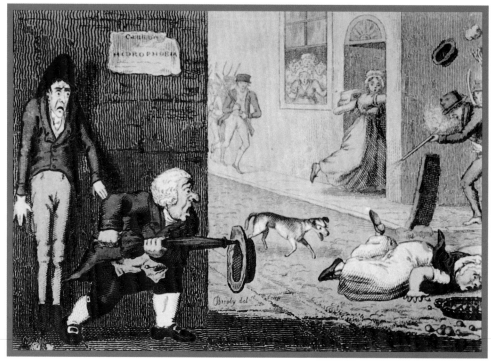

▲ Rabies had terrorized communities for centuries until Pasteur developed a vaccine for it. This 1826 cartoon depicts a rabid dog, or one with rabies, loose on the streets of London.

Twelve days later, on May 17, the animals were reinoculated with a stronger culture. Finally, on May 31, all of the immunized animals were infected with a highly virulent, or strong, anthrax culture. At the same time, a new group of animals that included twenty-four sheep, four cows, and one goat, were injected with the virulent anthrax culture.[5]

Two days later, on June 2, when Pasteur returned to the farm, all the vaccinated animals were well. Most of the unvaccinated animals were dead, while the rest were ill and would soon die. The crowd that had gathered, which included a reporter from a newspaper in London, was amazed. Before long, the world would learn of Pasteur's incredible scientific achievement.

⊝ PASTEUR'S RABIES VACCINE

With his vaccine for anthrax, Pasteur had conclusively proved that animals could be immunized against infectious disease. His new goal was to create a vaccine for a disease that affected humans.

In 1882, Pasteur began to study rabies. "I have always been haunted by the cries of those victims

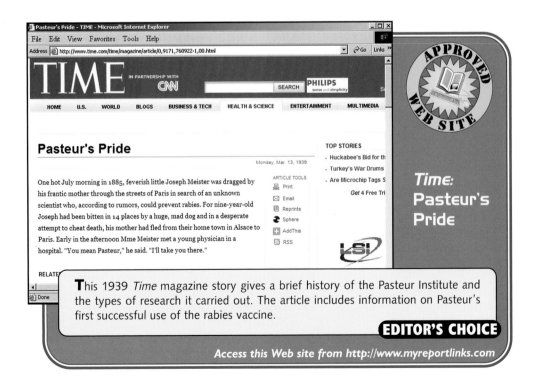

Pasteur's Pride - TIME - Microsoft Internet Explorer

File   Edit   View   Favorites   Tools   Help

Address http://www.time.com/time/magazine/article/0,9171,760922-1,00.html   Go   Links

TIME IN PARTNERSHIP WITH CNN   SEARCH   **PHILIPS** *sense and simplicity*

HOME   U.S.   WORLD   BLOGS   BUSINESS & TECH   HEALTH & SCIENCE   ENTERTAINMENT   MULTIMEDIA

Pasteur's Pride

Monday, Mar. 13, 1939

One hot July morning in 1885, feverish little Joseph Meister was dragged by his frantic mother through the streets of Paris in search of an unknown scientist who, according to rumors, could prevent rabies. For nine-year-old Joseph had been bitten in 14 places by a huge, mad dog and in a desperate attempt to cheat death, his mother had fled from their home town in Alsace to Paris. Early in the afternoon Mme Meister met a young physician in a hospital. "You mean Pasteur," he said. "I'll take you there."

TOP STORIES
. Huckabee's Bid for th
. Turkey's War Drums
. Are Microchip Tags S
    Get 4 Free Tri

ARTICLE TOOLS
🖨 Print
✉ Email
📑 Reprints
🔗 Sphere
➕ AddThis
📶 RSS

Time: **Pasteur's Pride**

This 1939 *Time* magazine story gives a brief history of the Pasteur Institute and the types of research it carried out. The article includes information on Pasteur's first successful use of the rabies vaccine.

EDITOR'S CHOICE

Access this Web site from http://www.myreportlinks.com

▲ Nine-year-old Joseph Meister was brought to Pasteur after a dog infected with rabies had bitten him. He was the first person to be successfully vaccinated against rabies.

of the mad wolf that came down the street of Arbois when I was a little boy,"[6] he said. So despite the fact that rabies was a fairly rare disease, the memory of the horrible pain it caused those who contracted it convinced Pasteur that he needed to help.

Pasteur and his partner, Dr. Roux, knew that the rabies virus affected an animal's brain and spinal cord, but they couldn't isolate the germ that caused the disease. Roux suggested a radical idea: Why not inject the virus directly into the brain of a healthy animal by means of trephination, the ancient practice of drilling a hole in a patient's head? Pasteur was horrified and said no. Roux went ahead anyway. Within a few weeks, the dog died, but the experiment convinced the scientists that they could cultivate the virus in the brains of lab animals and, thus, develop a vaccine.

⇒ JOSEPH MEISTER

Over the course of the next few years, while the scientists worked on other mysteries, they continued to experiment with rabies, growing the virus in rabbits and then weakening it by drying the affected nerve tissue. Finally, in 1884, Pasteur produced a vaccine. They experimented by transferring the rabies from infected animals to healthy ones. They placed spinal cord tissue from the sick

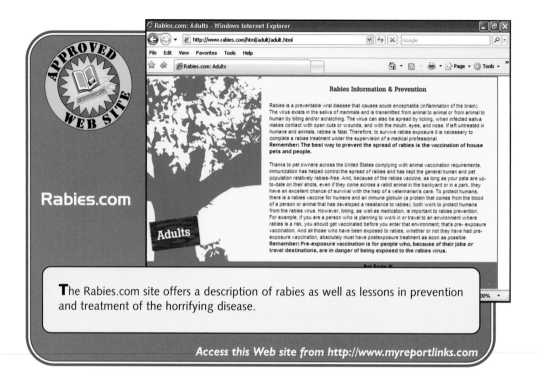

The Rabies.com site offers a description of rabies as well as lessons in prevention and treatment of the horrifying disease.

animals in direct contact with the brains of the healthy animals.

Pasteur and Roux then vaccinated an animal that already had rabies to see if the vaccine protected the infected animal. They repeated the experiment many times until they were sure the process worked. Now they needed to vaccinate a person to see if their method would protect humans who had been bit by a rabid animal.

In July 1885, nine-year-old Joseph Meister was brought to Pasteur's laboratory in Paris. Joseph had been attacked by a rabid dog, and his parents were afraid he would die. Pasteur vaccinated the boy, and he survived. Meister was the first person to be successfully vaccinated against rabies.

News of Pasteur's successful development of a rabies vaccine spread quickly. People who had been bitten by rabid animals began showing up at Pasteur's laboratory. By the end of that year, he had successfully vaccinated eighty people.

More and more people came to Pasteur for help, and he realized that his small laboratory was no longer big enough. He needed a full-scale clinic. Private donations provided the necessary funds and on November 14, 1888, the Pasteur Institute opened in Paris, with Pasteur as its director. When it opened, its purpose was to vaccinate people against rabies. However, Pasteur had bigger dreams for his Institute: He hoped that one day it would become a leading teaching and research center studying microbes and their connection to infectious diseases.

A Lasting Legacy

Louis Pasteur, the father of microbiology, died on September 28, 1895. He was eighty-three years old. On October 5, thousands of Parisians joined a huge funeral procession that made its way from the Pasteur Institute to the Cathedral of Notre Dame, where the funeral was held. Felix Faure, the President of France, and several foreign leaders attended.

Over the course of his brilliant career, Pasteur was one of the first scientists to grasp the connections between biology, chemistry, medicine, and health. Indeed, Pasteur summed up his vision when he said, "The object of scientific research is the improvement of human health."[1] His work in experimental and preventive medicine launched the modern age of medicine and gave birth to the science of microbiology.

CHAPTER

7

His research and experiments helped give rise t
diverse fields ranging from stereochemistry t
bacteriology to immunology to virology an
molecular biology.

Pasteur was one of the first scientist
to appreciate the importance of prac
tical applications of science to area
like agriculture, medicine, and indus
try. His many discoveries would contribute to a
increase in the average life span, from about fift
years in Pasteur's lifetime to about seventy-six now
Pasteurization, his method of killing bacteria i
liquid, led to the elimination of contaminated mil
and other drinks as sources of disease. Over time
other physicians came to accept his method o
immunization, which eventually resulted in contro
ling other deadly diseases like typhus and polio.

Pasteur is justifiably honored throughout th
world—today, streets, schools, hospitals, and labo
ratories throughout France and in many othe

Pasteur's thirst for knowledge and his appreciation for hard work led him to many great discoveries. He is justly remembered as one of the greatest inventors in history.

countries are named for him. However, more recently, historians have begun to take a more critical look at him and some of his accomplishments.

During his lifetime, Pasteur angered many of his peers in the scientific and medical communities—for example, a few in particular never forgave him for his assertions in 1864 that the theory of spontaneous generation was an error. Indeed, Pasteur could be arrogant and he was incredibly protective of and secretive about his work, so much so that in 1878, he made it clear to his family that the contents of his meticulous notebooks should be kept private—preferably forever.

As it happened, those notebooks did remain private for almost eighty years, until 1971, when

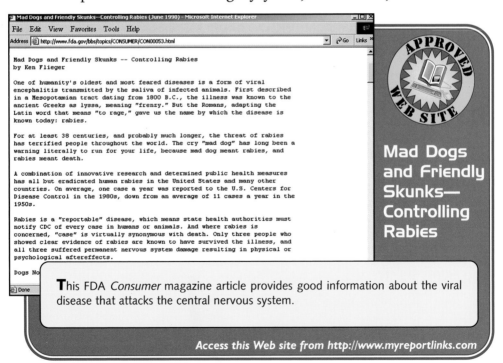

Mad Dogs and Friendly Skunks— Controlling Rabies

This FDA *Consumer* magazine article provides good information about the viral disease that attacks the central nervous system.

Access this Web site from http://www.myreportlinks.com

▲ On his seventieth birthday in 1892, the Sorbonne University honored Pasteur for his lifetime of service to France and his many contributions to science.

René Vallery-Radot, Pasteur's grandson and guardian of the notebooks, died. And despite their historical value—they are an encyclopedia of Pasteur's entire career—it would be a few more years still before anyone spent any real time analyzing them.

But in the 1990s, as the 100th anniversary of Pasteur's death approached, some historians began to study them, hoping to gain a better understanding of Pasteur's methods. And what they discovered in Pasteur's incredible written record were some clues that indicated Pasteur hadn't always been honest about what, exactly, some of his many laboratory experiments proved. In other words, his notebooks sometimes indicated one thing while Pasteur's public statements about the results of a given experiment sometimes said another.[2]

Since his death, Pasteur has come to be regarded as a hero; but it's also important to remember that he was also a human being, with faults just like the rest of us. Did he make mistakes? Absolutely. But no matter what his notebooks reveal or what else we might learn about him, not even his harshest critics deny the fact that Louis Pasteur was one of the greatest scientists who ever lived.

EXPERIMENTS WITH CRYSTALS AND MOLD

Follow in the footsteps of Louis Pasteur and try these experiments. Whether you do these experiments or others, remember that they should only be attempted under the supervision of a knowledgeable and responsible adult.

ACTIVITY #1

 **GROW YOUR OWN CRYSTALS**

Pasteur's first important scientific discoveries resulted from his research and experiments with crystals.

→ MATERIALS

- **powdered alum** (you can find this in your local supermarket in the spice section)
- **water**
- **a small pan**
- **a wooden spoon**
- **food coloring (green, red, yellow, blue)**
- **several small jars**

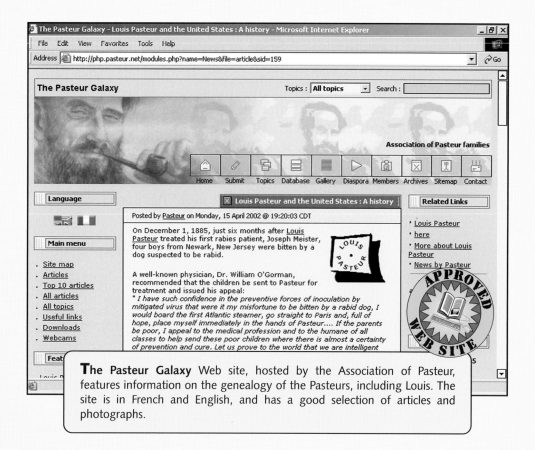

The Pasteur Galaxy Web site, hosted by the Association of Pasteur, features information on the genealogy of the Pasteurs, including Louis. The site is in French and English, and has a good selection of articles and photographs.

- **paper towels**
- **magnifying glass**

→ PROCEDURE

When you dissolve alum in boiling water, the alum grows crystals that look like gems. After adding the following ingredients, you will need to boil the mixture on the stove.

1. Measure 4 teaspoons of water and 3 teaspoons of powdered alum into the pan.

2. Add drops of food coloring to get crystals with specific colors. Try each of the following

ideas as separate procedures. Be sure to clean the pan and spoon thoroughly before trying each new color.

3. To get emerald crystals, add 10 drops of green food coloring.

4. To get ruby crystals, add 12 drops of red food coloring.

5. To get topaz crystals, add 10 drops of yellow food coloring.

6. To get sapphire crystals, add 10 drops of blue food coloring.

7. To get amber crystals, add 6 drops of yellow, 2 drops of red, and 1 drop of green food coloring.

8. If you do not add any food coloring, you will get colorless "diamond" crystals.

9. Bring the mixture to a boil, stirring for a few seconds until all of the alum is dissolved.

10. Allow the mixture to cool for two minutes.

11. Pour the alum solution into a jar and let it sit uncovered and undisturbed for three days. Be careful not to move the jar. Crystals will soon begin forming at the bottom of the jar.

After three days, carefully remove the crystals from the jar. Spread them out on a paper towel to dry. Use a magnifying glass to study the structure of the crystals.[1]

Activity #2

→ Create a Mold Terrarium

Some of Pasteur's most important scientific discoveries about bacteria and molds came from his research on the fermentation process. Pasteur showed that spoilage of wine, beer, milk, cheese, and other foods is caused by the growth of contaminating microorganisms that are carried by particles of dust in the air.

→ Materials

- **leftover food** (cheese, bread, cookies, cake, fruits, vegetables; do not use meat or fish

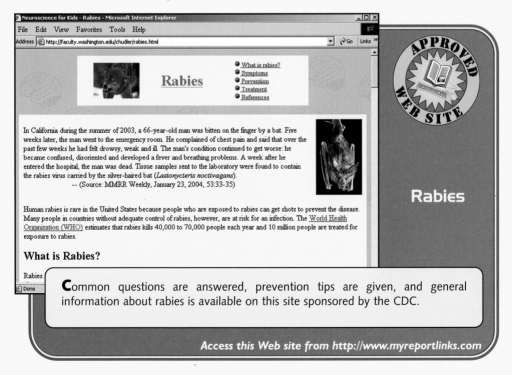

Neuroscience for Kids - Rabies - Microsoft Internet Explorer

File   Edit   View   Favorites   Tools   Help

Address http://faculty.washington.edu/chudler/rabies.html

Rabies

- What is rabies?
- Symptoms
- Prevention
- Treatment
- References

In California during the summer of 2003, a 66-year-old man was bitten on the finger by a bat. Five weeks later, the man went to the emergency room. He complained of chest pain and said that over the past few weeks he had felt drowsy, weak and ill. The man's condition continued to get worse: he became confused, disoriented and developed a fever and breathing problems. A week after he entered the hospital, the man was dead. Tissue samples sent to the laboratory were found to contain the rabies virus carried by the silver-haired bat (*Lasionycteris noctivagans*).
-- (Source: MMRR Weekly, January 23, 2004, 53:33-35)

Human rabies is rare in the United States because people who are exposed to rabies can get shots to prevent the disease. Many people in countries without adequate control of rabies, however, are at risk for an infection. The World Health Organization (WHO) estimates that rabies kills 40,000 to 70,000 people each year and 10 million people are treated for exposure to rabies.

What is Rabies?

Rabies

Done

Rabies

Common questions are answered, prevention tips are given, and general information about rabies is available on this site sponsored by the CDC.

Access this Web site from http://www.myreportlinks.com

leftovers because these would smell awful after a few days).

- **water**
- **a clear plastic container with a lid**
- **adhesive tape**

→ PROCEDURE

Use small pieces of leftover food (cut any big pieces into chunks about one inch square).

Dip each piece of food into some water and then put it into the plastic container. Arrange the pieces of food so that they are close to each other, but not touching.

Put the lid on the container. Then seal the container by putting adhesive tape around the edge of the lid. You have now created your mold terrarium, a clear plastic or glass container usually used to grow plants or to examine or hold small creatures.

Put your mold terrarium in a safe place where nobody will knock it over or throw it away.

Check your terrarium every day. After about three days, you should see blue, green, or white fuzzy material growing on some of the pieces of leftover food. The fuzzy stuff is mold, a kind of fungus. The mold grows from microorganisms, tiny spores that float around in the air. When spores land on a piece of damp food, they grow into mold.

Continue to check your mold terrarium every day for about two weeks. You will see the food rot as the mold grows and spreads. The mold feeds itself by producing chemicals that make the food break down and rot. (Certain foods that contain preservatives, such as a packaged cupcake, may only get slightly moldy.)

When the experiment is over, be sure to throw your mold terrarium in the garbage. Do not open the lid, because breathing or smelling the contents can cause some people to get sick.[2]

Report Links

The Internet sites described below can be accessed at http://www.myreportlinks.com

▶**Nobelprize.org: The Pasteur Institute**
Editor's Choice The Nobel Foundation has a good history of the Pasteur Institute.

▶**Pasteur Foundation**
Editor's Choice This organization supports scientific research and development.

▶*Time*: **Pasteur's Pride**
Editor's Choice This *Time* magazine article from 1939 features the Pasteur Institute.

▶**Louis Pasteur**
Editor's Choice This site provides a detailed outline of Pasteur's career.

▶**Wellcome Library**
Editor's Choice This library is an international resource for students of medical history.

▶**Immunization Timeline**
Editor's Choice This timeline focuses on significant milestones in the history of vaccination.

▶**Access Excellence @ The National Health Museum: Biotech Chronicles**
Read profiles of the individuals who helped build the biotechnology industry.

▶**Antiqua Medicina: From Homer to Vesalius**
The University of Virginia presents a series of essays on ancient medicine.

▶**"Apostles of the Germ"**
This is a fascinating look at germs and infectious diseases.

▶*Discover*: **Vital Signs**
Discover magazine has an article on rabies.

▶*The Dream and Lie of Louis Pasteur*
Originally written in 1942, this book alleges that Pasteur stole some of his ideas.

▶**Hippocratic Oath: Classical Version**
Read the classical version of the Hippocratic Oath on this PBS Web site.

▶**History in Focus: Medical History**
This site provides a variety of links to sources on the history of medicine.

▶**HowStuffWorks: What are Homogenization and Pasteurization?**
This Web site gives an overview of the processes of homogenization and pasteurization.

▶**Infectious Diseases Society of America**
This organization focuses on the prevention of infectious diseases.

Report Links

The Internet sites described below can be accessed at http://www.myreportlinks.com

▶**Louis Pasteur: Father of Modern Microbiology and Inventor of the First Vaccines for Animals**
This short article highlights Pasteur's career.

▶**Mad Dogs and Friendly Skunks—Controlling Rabies**
This FDA *Consumer* magazine article looks at the history of rabies.

▶**Modern History Sourcebook: Louis Pasteur (1822–1895)**
"Modern History Sourcebook" offers the reader this historical text about Louis Pasteur.

▶**NNDB: Louis Pasteur**
This is a biography of Louis Pasteur.

▶**The Pasteur Galaxy**
The Association of Pasteur's Web site on the history and genealogy of Pasteur families.

▶**Rabies**
Get important rabies information on this Web site.

▶**Rabies.com**
This University of Washington Web site has good information on rabies.

▶**Red Gold: Hippocrates**
This PBS site has a biography of Hippocrates.

▶**The Royal Society**
An independent organization that promotes excellence in science.

▶**Science, "Society", and Immunity**
Modern Drug Discovery's article on the evolution of vaccines and anti-toxins.

▶**The Scientific Underpinnings of the 1906 Pure Food and Drugs Act: Microbe Mania**
Using excerpts from *Puck* magazine, this article provides a historical look at germs.

▶**Timeline Science: One Thousand Years of Scientific Thought**
Explore the scientific accomplishments of the last one thousand years.

▶**Stop That Germ!**
This long *Time* magazine article focuses on bacteria, vaccines, and immunology.

▶*A Traveler's Guide to the History of Biology and Medicine*
This travel book takes you to the site of some international medical milestones.

▶**World Wide School: The Evolution of Modern Medicine**
This set of lectures was delivered at Yale University in April 1913.

anthrax—A disease that affects sheep, cattle, and other animals and that can be spread to humans.

bacteria—A type of microorganism; some bacteria cause disease, others do not.

crystal—One of the regularly shaped objects that many substances form when they harden.

culture—A colony of microorganisms grown in a special substance for scientific study.

fermentation—A gradual chemical change in which sugar is changed into alcohol and carbon dioxide gas.

germ—A microbe.

germ theory—The theory that states that fermentation and certain diseases are caused by specific microorganisms.

immunity—The body's resistance to a previously encountered disease-causing microbe.

infectious disease—A disease caused by a microbe that enters the body and reproduces; many infectious diseases can be spread from one person to another.

inoculate—To introduce pathogens, disease-causing organisms, into an organism to stimulate an immunity to a disease.

miasma—An atmosphere filled with vapor that was thought to have caused disease.

microbe—A microorganism that can cause disease.

microbiology—The branch of science that deals with microorganisms.

microorganism—An organism so small it can only be viewed through a microscope. Bacteria are one kind of microorganism.

molecule—A number of atoms joined together to form a stable and definite structure.

pasteurization—A process for heating milk or other liquids hot enough and long enough to kill harmful bacteria.

pathogen—An agent such as a bacterium or virus that causes disease.

rabies—A deadly disease that people can get from the bite of an infected animal.

smallpox—A serious disease that causes skin sores; smallpox has been nearly eradicated by vaccination.

spontaneous generation—The theory, now disproved, that living things arise from nonliving matter.

stereochemistry—The branch of science that deals with the spatial arrangement of atoms and molecules in a compound and how that arrangement affects the properties of the compound.

sterilization—A process of heating something to make it free of microorganisms.

theory—An explanation based on observation and reasoning.

vaccination—The giving of a preparation of weakened or killed microbes to a person or animal to prevent a disease.

virology—The branch of science that deals with the study of viruses and the diseases caused by them.

virulent—Extremely poisonous or disease-causing.

yeast—A type of microorganism that grows quickly in the presence of sugar.

Chapter 2. Early Beliefs About Disease

1. Bernice Essenfeld, Carol R. Gontang, and Randy Moore, *Biology* (Menlo Park, Calif.: Addison-Wesley Publishing Company, 1996), p. 319.

2. René J. Dubos, *Louis Pasteur: Free Lance of Science* (Boston: Little, Brown and Company, 1950), pp. 236–237.

3. Patrice Debré, *Louis Pasteur* (Baltimore: The Johns Hopkins University Press, 1998), p. 296.

4. Dubos, p. 237.

5. Debré, p. 296.

Chapter 3. The Early Years

1. Patrice Debré, *Louis Pasteur* (Baltimore: The Johns Hopkins University Press, 1998), p. 9.

2. Ibid., p. 8.

3. Ibid., p. 9.

4. Ibid., p. 12.

5. René J. Dubos, *Louis Pasteur: Free Lance of Science* (Boston: Little, Brown and Company, 1950), p. 27.

6. Dubos, p. 27.

7. Paul de Kruif, *Microbe Hunters* (Harcourt, Brace and Company, Inc., 1926), pp. 59–60.

Chapter 4. A Scientist Is Born

1. J.T. Merz, *A History of European Thought in the Nineteenth Century* (New York: Dover Publications, 1965), pp. 404–405

2. Patrice Debré, *Louis Pasteur* (Baltimore: The Johns Hopkins University Press, 1998), pp. 50–51.

Chapter 5. Focusing on Fermentation

1. Patrice Debré, *Louis Pasteur* (Baltimore: The Johns Hopkins University Press, 1998), p. 54.

2. René J. Dubos, *Louis Pasteur: Free Lance of Science* (Boston: Little, Brown and Company, 1950), p. 38.

3. Emile Roux, as appears in Debré, p. 57.

4. Louis Pasteur, "Quotation," as posted on QuotationsBooks.com, 2007, <http://www.QuotationsBook.com/quote/35230/> (January 28, 2008).

5. Paul de Kruif, *Microbe Hunters* (Harcourt, Brace and Company, Inc., 1926), p. 64

6. Debré, p. 124.

7. Ibid., p. 148

8. Jan Baptista van Helmont, as posted at "An Initial Overview of Ecology," Warner College of Natural Resources, n.d., <http://welcome.warnercnr.colostate.edu/class_info/ey505/505week1.htm> (January 28, 2008).

9. René Vallery-Radot, *The Life of Pasteur* (Dover Publications, Inc., 1960), pp. 108–109

Chapter 6. Dangerous Microorganisms

1. René J. Dubos, *Louis Pasteur: Free Lance of Science* (Boston: Little, Brown and Company, 1950), p. 218.

2. Pasteur, Joubert et Chamberland, *La théorie des germes et ses applications à la médecine et à la chirurgie*, Bulletin de l'Académie de médecine, 2e série, t. 7, 1878, p. 446

3. Patrice Debré, *Louis Pasteur* (Baltimore: The Johns Hopkins University Press, 1998), p. 337.

4. Paul de Kruif, *Microbe Hunters* (Harcourt, Brace and Company, Inc., 1926), p. 154

5. Dubos, pp. 339–340.

6. de Kruif, p. 170

Chapter 7. A Lasting Legacy

1. Patrice Debré, *Louis Pasteur* (Baltimore: The Johns Hopkins University Press, 1998), p. 499.

2. Gerald L. Geison, *The Private Science of Louis Pasteur* (Princeton: Princeton University Press, 1995).

Experiments With Crystals and Mold

1. "Try This! Fun Science," n.d., *National Geographic Kids,* <http://www.nationalgeographic.com/ngkids/trythis/tryfun1.html> (April 26, 2007).

2. "Science Explorer: Mold Terrarium," *The Exploratorium,* n.d., <http://www.exploratorium.edu/science_explorer/mold.html> (April 26, 2007).

Ackerman, Jane. *Louis Pasteur and the Founding of Microbiology.* Greensboro, N.C.: Morgan Reynolds Publishing, 2004.

Alphin, Elaine Marie. *Germ Hunter: A Story About Louis Pasteur.* Minneapolis: Carolrhoda Books, 2003.

Birch, Beverly. *Louis Pasteur: Father of Modern Medicine.* San Diego: Blackbirch Press, 2001.

Fandel, Jennifer. *Louis Pasteur and Pasteurization.* Mankato, Minn.: Capstone Press, 2007.

Gogerly, Liz. *Louis Pasteur.* Austin, Tex.: Raintree Steck-Vaughn, 2002.

Lassieur, Allison. *Louis Pasteur: Revolutionary Scientist.* New York: Franklin Watts, 2005.

Phelan, Glen. *Killing Germs, Saving Lives: The Quest for the First Vaccines.* Washington, D.C.: National Geographic, 2007.

Robbins, Louise. *Louis Pasteur and the Hidden World of Microbes.* New York: Oxford University Press, 2001.

Silverthorne, Elizabeth. *Louis Pasteur.* Farmington Hills, Mich.: Lucent Books, 2004.

Smith, Linda Wasmer. *Louis Pasteur: Disease Fighter.* Berkeley Heights, N.J.: Enslow Publishers, 2008.

Snedden, Robert. *Scientists and Discoveries.* Chicago: Heinemann Library, 2007.